THE BICYCLE

THE BICYCLE

A Guide & Manual R John Way

Hamlyn
London New York Sydney Toronto

Acknowledgments

The drawings throughout this book were prepared by
the author, R. John Way. The publishers are also grateful
to the following organizations and individuals for photographs:
Bicycle Institute of America Inc; Hamlyn Group Library;
A.J. King; Peter Knottley; Geoffrey Magnay; Bernard Thompson.

Published by The Hamlyn Publishing Group Limited,
London · New York · Sydney · Toronto
Hamlyn House, Feltham, Middlesex, England
Copyright © The Hamlyn Publishing Group Limited, 1973

ISBN 0 600 31784 6

Printed in Great Britain by Sir Joseph Causton and Sons Limited

Contents

Introduction

More years ago than I care to remember I was walking along a lane on a crisp winter's morning when three cyclists came by, smoothly pedalling their low fixed gears, and disappeared silently into the distance. It may seem a very small incident but from that moment I wanted to become a cyclist–I had no ideas of racing or touring, I just wanted to ride.

It is quite likely that you have other reasons. One of the real joys of the bicycle is its ability to satisfy youthful enthusiasms for competitive sport, and after these have been dissipated, it is still there to help you find new pleasures. Bicycling can be a lifelong hobby at different levels, and in varying intensities, and with some luck it will be one you will not have to give up because of increasing age. We all want something for nothing, or at the very least, a good bargain. When I decided I wanted to ride a bicycle,

it did not occur to me for one moment that I might be enriching my mind as I rode through the land, or that my body would benefit from the activity.

Times have changed. The reputation of Dr. Paul Dudley White has spread far beyond the shores of the U.S.A. Many desk-bound or auto-enslaved folk are looking to the bicycle in the hope that it will enable them to keep some sort of contact between their mind and body. It is my hope that in doing this they will discover the real joy of just riding a bicycle, suiting the route to their mood, and the effort to their ability, and not just as some form of medicine.

In this book I have tried to provide a balanced background to the bicycle, its history, its mechanism and the sport which is built around it. There are excellent volumes which deal with each of these aspects in greater detail than is possible

here, and if your acquaintance with the bicycle is more than superficial, I urge you to seek them out. The budding racing man in particular will find it advantageous to learn from experience rather than experiment.

Bicycling can be so rewarding a pursuit that you may never want for the company of others, but there is much to be said for membership of a cycling club, if only for occasional companionship. When my own club promotes open races, elderly members can be seen assisting in the organization, perhaps repaying a little of the debt most of us owe this wonderful activity.

To be able to traverse one's country giving offence to no one, seeing, hearing, and smelling all that nature has to offer, is unique in this pollution-ridden age. You just need a bicycle. I hope this book helps you to choose the right one.

Dr. Paul Dudley White, whose enthusiasm has encouraged many Americans to take up bicycling as a healthy recreation.

The Story of the Bicycle

Records of manumotive vehicles go back to the Middle Ages, to Giovanni Fontana of Padua, who in 1418 designed a four-wheeled vehicle propelled by the driver who pulled an endless rope connected via gears to the wheels. Soon after I acquired my first lightweight bicycle, my father suggested that I should make a pilgrimage to Stoke Poges church in Buckinghamshire, to see what he described as the first record of man riding a bicycle. This is depicted on a stained glass window made in 1642, and one is left to guess what the rear end of the device might have looked like.

Our interest is with real bicycles, however, and the first known vehicle with two wheels in one track was introduced by Comte de Sivrac in 1791. This was simply a wooden horse with two wheels. There was no steering system and it was propelled, initially in the gardens of the Palais Royal, by pushing alternate feet backwards against the ground. If you have tried to ride a bicycle with the steering locked you will appreciate that it must have been difficult to balance one of these devices. By the mid 1790s the velocifère, as it had become known, was quite popular, largely as a sort of adult toy – indeed it had probably been inspired in the first place by a child's plaything. Races were run down the Champs-Elysées, but it does not seem to have had any practical use. In 1816 an improved version was demonstrated in the Luxembourg Gardens by Nicephore Niepce, more famous for an eight-hour exposure of his lunch in 1822 which was probably the world's first photograph. This machine did not at first have steering, but it may have been added later.

The bicycle which appeared a year later certainly did have steering. This was the work of Baron von Drais of Mannheim, an engineer who needed a vehicle to go about his business. The wooden spoked wheels were mounted in a semi-triangulated frame, on top of which was a padded saddle, and a raised rest. This supported the arms, and helped when thrusting backwards with the feet. It became known as a Draisiènne, dandy horse, or hobby horse, and judging by contemporary accounts was capable of speeds up to 10 mph. *Ackermann's Magazine* even hinted

This stained glass window is in the Buckinghamshire church of Stoke Poges, which is more widely famous for its connection with Thomas Gray, who is reputed to have written his Elegy in its churchyard.

that the exercise was beneficial, and that was a good few years before Dr. Paul Dudley White! Within a year, a ladies' version was introduced. The Draisiènne soon became popular in France, and the enthusiasm spread to Germany, Britain and the United States. It was not long before an accessory appeared, a mileometer operated by the back wheel, becoming available in 1825.

The hobby horse gradually lost its appeal. It was, after all, largely a fashion and it was the transformation of its means of propulsion by Kirkpatrick Macmillan, a Scottish blacksmith, that produced the first really practical bicycle. This achievement is all the more remarkable because Macmillan did not just fix treadles and cranks to a hobby horse. His machine bore more than a passing resemblance to the safety bicycle. But it was built in 1839 and 30 years were to pass before a hint of the first safety was to appear. Some of the shapes which were to arrive in the years between, may at first seem strange, but it must be remembered that gearing was direct and in consequence related to the driving wheel's diameter, which was the only variable available to the builder.

The next decade seems to have found little inspiration in Macmillan's design, and instead tricycles and quadricycles were developed. These were usually treadle driven, were heavy and in many cases were completely without brakes.

In 1861 a hobby horse with pedals emerged from the workshops of the Michaux brothers, who were manufacturers of perambulators and tricycles. Apparently a customer had taken this machine for repair, and the father of the family suggested fitting cranks to the front wheel – one wonders what the owner had to say when he came to collect his repaired machine. Michaux had in his employ a mechanic, one Pierre Lallement, who claimed responsibility for this work, although nobody seems to be sure if there is any truth in his story.

A German, Karl Kech, also hit on this idea quite independently, but did nothing to exploit it, and it was left to the Michaux firm to go into production with the first pedal-driven bicycle. Lallement left the firm soon after this and in 1866 went to America where in conjunction with James Carrol he took out the first U.S. cycle patent.

By the mid 1860s Michaux' 'boneshakers' were being sold in large numbers. An Englishman, Rowley Turner, became an enthusiast for them while a student in Paris and when he became the Paris agent for the Coventry Sewing Machine Co., he suggested that his firm should build these bicycles to supplement French production, which could not keep pace with the demand. The firm's name was changed to the Coventry Machinists Co. Ltd., and thus the foundations of the most important centre of the industry were laid.

By the late 1860s established designs were in large-scale production and improved versions of components began to appear. In America the Hanlon brothers invented the slotted crank which gave the rider a choice in the length of throw. Wire spokes made their first appearance in 1866, although these were not the threaded adjustable kind in use today. In the search for better performance, front wheels, which were still the driven ones, were increased in diameter, and in 1868 rubber shod wheels were first fitted.

In many ways France dominated this era, and in 1869 the first cycle show was held in Paris. Crude freewheels and variable gears were displayed, while rubber tyres, tubular frames, sprung wheels, and band brakes were among the exhibits. In the same year André Guilmet, a French clockmaker, designed what must have been the first safety bicycle (which still exists). Its inventor was killed in the Franco-Prussian war; because his machine contained so many innovations, yet was not exploi-

ted commercially, some doubt still hangs over its authenticity. Although possessing the backbone frame and saddle arrangement of the Michaux boneshaker, it had wire spokes, rubber tyres, and a chain driven rear wheel. In Britain that same year F. W. Shearing also published a safety bicycle design, but he did not bother to build or patent it.

The real introduction of the safety bicycle was still some years away, and the cult of the ordinary, 'penny farthing' or high bicycle, began to develop.

Driving wheels became larger, varying in diameter between 40in and 60in. This not only provided higher gearing, but a more comfortable ride into the bargain. As a standard ordinary weighed about 50lb there was plenty of scope for refinement, and racing ordinaries could be made at half this figure. The Windsor illustrated on page 15, is a beautifully made example from a small maker.

In looking for the origins of the refinements to machines in the early 1870s one name appears continually – James Starley. His tie rod method of spoke tensioning, introduced on the Ariel in 1870, worked by turning the hub in relation to its rim. The following year he fitted this machine with a 2:1 gear, and in 1872 further modified his spoking system; ultimately in 1877 he introduced the tangent system we know today. A radially-spoked driving wheel tends to be spongy because the hub can turn in relation to its rim. Tensioning produced other solutions (among them, the earliest ordinary, made by Reynold and Mays in 1869, had hub flanges which could be moved farther apart in order to tighten the wheel). The method by which we true our wheels today was discovered by W. H. J. Grout in 1871. He introduced not only threaded spokes, but also hollow rubber tyres which were vulcanised to the rim, hollow front forks, and pedals.

The problem of gearing for ordinaries taxed other minds than

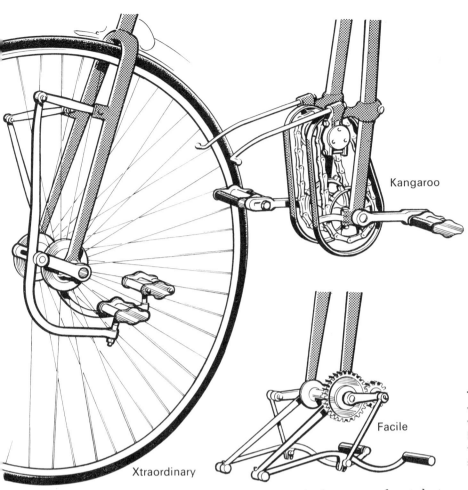

Kangaroo

Facile

Xtraordinary

These variations on the ordinary were some of the methods by which saddles could be moved back, and wheels made smaller, with improvements in speed and safety.

Starley's and there were many interesting solutions. Apart from increasing the gearing it was obviously an advantage to reduce the front wheel to a more manageable size, and once this was achieved it also became possible to position the pedals more satisfactorily, and this in turn brought the saddle farther aft. The Facile drive illustrated was patented in 1869 but was not used until 1878. The 24 hour record was broken in 1883 on one of these machines, when J. H. Adams covered $242\frac{1}{2}$ miles. Both the Facile and Singer's Xtraordinary used a lever system in which the pedals went up and down in an arc. On the other hand, the Kangaroo, produced by Hillman, Herbert and Cooper, used a chain drive. The end of the 1870s saw the introduction of ball and roller bearings, which replaced the plain and conical types.

An interestingly original development of the ordinary was the American Star. Here the small wheel was at the front, and was the steerable one. The drive sys-

tem was via levers and ratchets. Because these were independently mounted it was not necessary for them to be diametrically opposed – for a quick standing start it might have been an advantage to push them both down at the same time! The Star appeared in 1880.

While ordinary design was being refined in the 1870s, the tricycle was also being developed. The earliest form was a modified boneshaker and was known as the German tricycle (curiously, some hundred years later, British riders who want a cheap tricycle often convert a bicycle by fitting a special double rear wheel unit). The single front wheel drive of the Michaux was retained, and in the Dublin tricycle, another early type, the single drive was placed at the rear, and both front wheels were steerable. The American answer to the problem in the Topliff and Ely machine was to make it possible to vary the track of the wheels from 2in to 2ft – while on the move! In 1877 James Starley brought out the Coventry lever

Top, left to right: By the application of steering to the hobby horse, Baron von Drais turned it into a practical form of transport; the machine he designed in 1817 was known as a Draisiènne. Kirkpatrick Macmillan was the first man to make a bicycle with a driving mechanism, and this treadle-operated design appeared in 1839. Michaux' boneshaker of 1861 was basically a hobby horse with pedals directly connected to the front wheel. The design soon became popular and cycling, as a social activity and a competitive sport, owes much to its introduction. The Phantom ordinary of Reynold and Mays, which appeared in 1869, was a great improvement on the boneshaker. It employed a triangulated frame and tension spoked wheels. Spoke tensioning was achieved by increasing the separation of the hub flanges.

Left: This treadle-driven tricycle is typical of many machines produced in the 1850s. It was very heavy, and lacking such refinements as brakes, was far from practical. The drive operated through only one of the rear wheels.

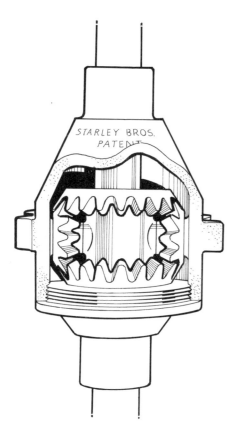

STARLEY BROS. PATENT

Starley's differential made driving both side wheels of a tricycle a practical proposition.

Right: Three stages in the development of the chain.

tricycle. This was a twin track machine, where the driving wheel was offset in a central position. Later the lever drive arrangement gave way to chain, and it became known as the Coventry Rotary. The tricycle lent itself readily to adaptation for the carriage of two riders and in 1882 Bayliss Thomas produced the first tandem tricycle. Sociables, where the riders sat side by side, appeared in various forms but this layout was not as practical as a fore and aft one.

The layout which eventually proved most popular for tricycles employed a single front steerable wheel. Unfortunately this meant that the drive had to be offset via one of the rear wheels. Again it was Starley who solved the problem, with a differential gear which in principle is the same as that used by the motor industry today. This idea soon became popular and was first used on his Royal Salvo machine in 1880. The Humber Cripper of 1884 with direct steering set the pattern for the future (the name Cripper was derived from a professional rider of the day, Bob Cripps, who raced one of them). At the same time several single rear wheel driving machines with twin steering were popular, but none remained in vogue.

Despite the designs of Guilmet and Shearing, the first safety bicycle to be built and ridden was H. J. Lawson's model of 1873. When a production version emerged in 1879 it was called the Bicyclette. The steering was indirect, the front wheel much larger than the rear driving wheel and the latter sported a mudguard. The design

does not seem to have achieved any commercial success. That was reserved for the Rover safety introduced in 1885. The first version of this machine had indirect steering like the Bicyclette, but this soon gave way to direct operation in the second version. Both these models had rather flimsy frames, particularly at the rear, but the third type (illustrated on page 19) had much stiffer seat stays, although the straight forks seemed a retrograde step. The machine weighed 37lb. The diamond frame which we know today was not produced until 1890, when it appeared on the Humber safety; their earlier machine of 1884, like the Rover, only lacked a seat tube.

The dreadful state of roads in the 19th Century encouraged the development of various forms of springing. Linley and Biggs with their Whippet had a well thought out design, for the saddle, pedals and handlebars kept their relative positions during deflection. This was made in 1885 and in 1887 a more basic design called the British Star appeared. Here a single coil spring behind the seat tube was compressed by the rear triangle, altering the relative position of the pedals. The Cremorne designer went as far as springing the front wheel via bottom links. The invention of the pneumatic tyre was to severely curtail experiments on these lines, however.

While chain drive seems an obvious way of transmitting power, the early types were far removed from the roller chain perfected by Hans Renold in the last 20 years of the century. In the

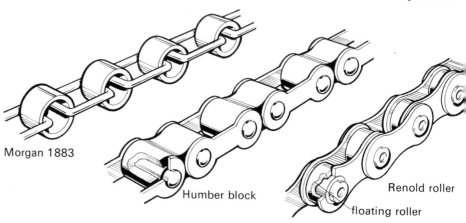

Morgan 1883

Humber block

Renold roller

floating roller

Facile, for example, the drive was based on that used in the ordinary of that name, designed by John Beale. A development, the geared Facile, interposed a sun and planet to reduce the pedalling rate. In 1891 the Crypto company, who had amalgamated with the producers of the Facile, Ellis and Co., introduced a front drive safety called the Bantam, on which the cranks were not connected directly to the hub but drove via an epicyclic gear.

Open frames are mainly restricted to ladies' bicycles, but before the diamond frame became universally popular, various cross-frame safety machines appeared. The Ivel of 1886 was of particular interest because its designer, one Dan Albone, anticipated most of the attempts in recent years to introduce a new kind of frame, based on recent technological developments. Humber made a similar type, incorporating chain stays in their design.

While these pioneering dev-elopments were taking place in Europe, a bicycle industry was being built up in the United States. Colonel Albert A. Pope of Boston started to import ordina-ries from Coventry in 1876, and when his factory went into pro-duction two years later bicycle-riding became a fashionable Amer-ican pastime. By the 1890s it had grown into a craze and by the end of the decade there were over 400 bicycle manufacturers. Col. Pope's factory, which produced Columbia bicycles, was one of the largest in the world, and pioneered mass production tech-niques. The Columbia safety which was produced in 1895 weighed only 24lb and was equip-ped with pneumatic tyres. One of Pope's representatives, inciden-tally once made an astonishing discovery in Alabama. A young negro who could not afford a bicycle set to and made one. What is more to wonder at is the originality of the design. The drive is via three gears, the rear

Discovered in Alabama in the 1890s, this early safety shows remarkable thinking.

Left: The Ariel of 1870 had a large driving wheel, which was necessary to achieve a practical gear ratio. Here the spokes are tensioned by tie rods, which twist the hubs.

Opposite: The Windsor ordinary, or Penny Farthing, is typical of high-quality bicycles built in the 1880s by small craftsman manufacturers. They were able to reduce the weight of their products considerably and a racing ordinary could be as light as 25 lb.

Opposite, right: The German tricycle was a modified boneshaker, and the example shown here was produced in the 1860s by a Mr. Lisle of Wolverhampton.

Opposite, below: The Coventry lever tricycle was the first really successful three wheeler—James Starley introduced it in 1877.

Below: The American Star, a popular racing machine, was propelled by cranks connected to ratchet mechanisms. By placing a small wheel at the front, a more satisfactory weight distribution was achieved.

one being made of wood with iron teeth. The drawing shows his novel method of saddle adjustment.

In 1896 Lu-mi-num, a St. Louis company, made a frame of aluminium which was licensed to be built in Britain. One of the very first acetylene lamps, the 20th Century, was produced in 1888, and one of the early tubeless tyre designs, by Lungren, was rideable even when deflated – the motor industry is just getting around to this idea.

Early bicycle wheels were iron shod, and resembled coach wheels. Solid, and later hollow, rubber tyres improved comfort but the introduction of pneumatic tyres in 1888 was to revolutionise the situation. Riders without these tyres were soon being given extra handicaps in races. A Dublin veterinary surgeon, John Boyd Dunlop, patented the application of these tyres for cycles, but the idea actually belongs to R. W. Thomson, whose design was aimed at the horse-drawn carriage. The success of Dunlop's tyres must have been hastened by the Du Cross brothers of Dublin, who raced on them so successfully. This first design was held in place by solution around the rim, and was about as inconvenient to mend as one could possibly imagine. Wired-on tyres –clinchers– were made possible by the inventions of C. K. Welch and W. E. Bartlett and developed for the Dunlop company. By 1895 any other form of tyre had virtually ceased to exist.

One of the most important developments in the early days of the pneumatic tyre was brought to Britain from America by J.F. Palmer. In 1892 he patented the cross ply tyre, in which parallel fibres were wound round the tube diagonally, with another layer on top at right angles to the first and a rubber bonding between the opposing fibres. This system reduced chaffing, and when later combined with the clincher principle, an ideal detachable tyre resulted.

As soon as the safety had become a reality, variable gearing began to appear in various forms. One of the earliest was a two chain system fitted to the Sparkbrook. This was an open frame safety design of 1887. Two years later S.J. Collier introduced a two-speed epicyclic bottom bracket gear. The ultimately successful epicyclic hub gear, the Sturmey Archer, was patented in 1902 and made by the Raleigh company. One of the earliest derailleur gears seems to have been that of Linley and Biggs. The four-speed Protean was patented in 1894, and their two-speed gear exhibited at the Stanley Show in 1900 used a wide chainwheel and a special chain, the whole thing sliding sideways rather than bending.

Below: The Gradient derailleur of 1899. A spring plate at the chainwheel is pulled round when back-pedalling. This operates two quadrant forks which pull the chain clear of the sprockets. These can be moved in either direction to engage a different gear. On pedalling forwards, the chain then drops back in place.

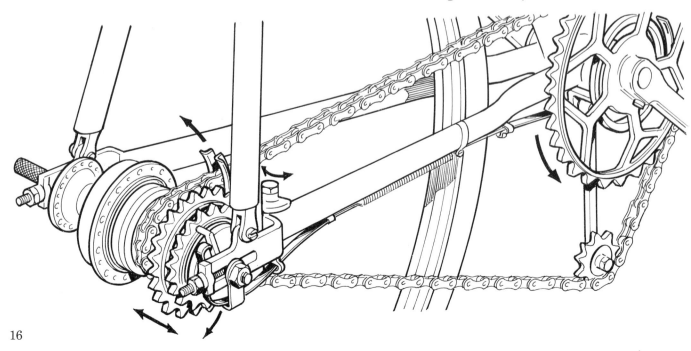

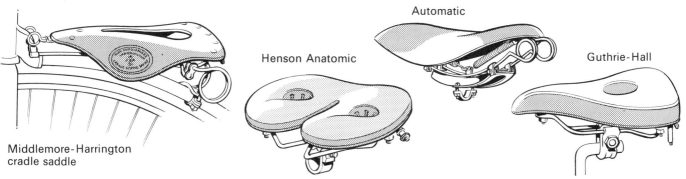

Automatic

Henson Anatomic

Guthrie-Hall

Middlemore-Harrington
cradle saddle

The Protean achieved its changes of gear via a split chainwheel. Pedalling backwards made it open, and it could be set in four positions. A freewheel was incorporated in the chainwheel, and a jockey took up chain tension. E. H. Hodgkinson's Gradient of 1899 more closely resembled the modern derailleur in design. It drove one of three cogs, and employed a chain tensioner which will remind some readers of the Osgear. The sketch shows its sequence of operation.

These early ancestors of the derailleur were looked on with scorn by most riders, who either preferred a single gear, or the admittedly superior engineering of epicyclic hubs. The derailleur gear much as we know it today originated in France in about 1910 when the retro-direct system also appeared. In this design two separate chain drives of different ratios are employed. Each has its own freewheel, and one of the systems works whilst pedalling forwards, the other when pedalling backwards. There is not really

much that can be said in its favour, apart for the absence of a control mechanism.

Quite early in the history of the bicycle, the now familiar saddle shape was evolved. Some were mounted on leaf springs, others hung between coil springs in the manner of a hammock, but most had wire frames, leather tops, and springs underneath. In the 1890s a number of 'anatomical saddles' appeared. These incorporated depressions or holes to relieve pressure, and to these ends pneumatic saddles were also made. The Guthrie-Hall and the Henson Anatomic were two of that type. One interesting saddle was the Automatic, designed so that the rider was able to alter its tilt whilst on the move.

As long as bicycles had solid tyres there was not much incentive to depart from the spoon brake which operated on to the top of the wheel. In the case of bicycles with no freewheel mechanisms, there was even less incentive. Even the spoon brake had to be treated with caution

when applied to the front wheel of an ordinary – it was all too easy to take a flyer! Starley produced a scissor action brake which perhaps later inspired the caliper type. The first machine to be fitted with brakes operating on to the rim was the New Whippet of 1897.

Early lamps used either candles or oil. The ordinary often appeared with its lamp suspended from the front hub, inside the spokes. Joseph Lucas started manufacturing cycle lamps in 1879 and in 1888 the American 20th Century acetylene lamp appeared. Ten years were to pass before Lucas brought their version out.

With the turn of the century, the development of the bicycle has become a history of refinement, culminating in today's highly efficient machines, which are as good to look at as they are to ride. Let us hope that modern technology does nothing to destroy this balance, as new materials make their impact on the industry.

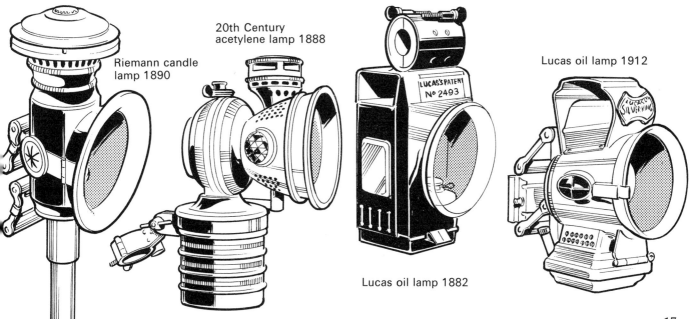

Riemann candle
lamp 1890

20th Century
acetylene lamp 1888

Lucas oil lamp 1912

LUCAS'S PATENT
No 2493

Lucas oil lamp 1882

Opposite, top: The Humber
Cripper tricycle of 1884.
Bottom: H.J. Lawson's
Bicyclette was the first safety
bicycle design to get off the
drawing board, appearing in
prototype form in 1873.

Left: James Starley's 1885 Rover
safety, the true forerunner of the
modern bicycle.

Top: The Linley and Biggs Whippet
of 1885.

Above: Dan Albone's cross frame
safety of 1886, the Ivel.

IVEL TRACTOR 1903
Dan Albone, Biggleswade, Beds.

Choosing a Bicycle

There was a time when a man bought a bicycle, put lamps on it to ride to work, strapped a bag on it for his holiday, and took very nearly everything off it when he entered a race. In the affluent society this is perhaps no longer necessary, but if you just want to ride around for the sheer pleasure of it, one bicycle will be enough. If riding gives you a taste for long distance touring and camping, it would be desirable to have a special bicycle for that alone, but it would certainly not be necessary. However, the racing man who indulges in time trials or massed starts just cannot get started on the track without putting his hand in his pocket. Some branches of the sport seem to demand a high degree of sophistication, yet I can remember some magnificent winning rides on bicycles which today would be spurned by the average schoolboy. If you can afford the best, then buy it for the pleasure it will bring, but do not be deterred if you have to be economical. The law of diminishing returns applies to bicycles, too.

The diagram which shows typical angles and dimensions for touring, road racing, and track frames, gives an outline of ideas of current thinking on the subject–there will be variations from one maker to another, but they will not be drastic. In the past some builders brought out designs with strangely shaped forks and stays, curved seat tubes, and enclosed brackets. It does seem, though, that the conventional frame takes a lot of beating. Most frames bought off the peg are made in sizes ranging from about 21 in to 24 in. This will suit the vast majority, but while some ranges go down to about $20\frac{3}{8}$ in, tall men are likely to need a specially built frame.

It is still quite feasible to use just one bicycle for weekday riding and touring, and perhaps even racing. A pair of racing wheels and a tough rear one with wider ratio cogs will make things easier, but it is possible to race on wired-on tyres (clinchers) if the money will not stretch to tubulars (sew-ups). The most practical frame will be the type used for road racing. It is not quite what a dedicated tourist would choose, but it will be near enough, and a normal racing derailleur is capable of meeting quite a wide range of requirements (the Simplex Prestige would be a good choice). The important thing to avoid in an all-purpose machine of this type is fitting anything specially suited to one type of riding–Randonneur bars, and long cranks which might suit the tourist and time trialist, for example, are less than ideal on a maid of all work.

There is a class of bicycle which one sees all too rarely and that is the town rider's mount. There are many areas which have no

Right: America's parks afford wonderful settings for road races.

These three frames give some idea of typical shapes for touring, road racing and track work.

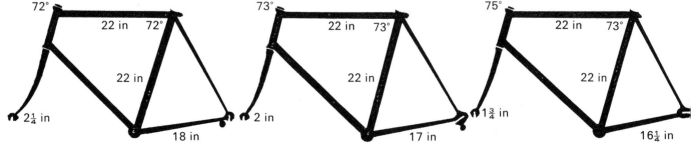

Above: The Moulton small wheel bicycle employs a rubber suspension system, and very high pressure tyres. It has been raced successfully and is a practical touring bicycle, but is perhaps best of all a town machine, easy to load and to use in traffic.

hills and where the cyclist is not out to break records. Derailleurs, toe clips and straps and the usual garnishes are just a waste of money and weight; a single gear, dynamo, rubber pedals, carrier with retaining spring and basket on the front would be quite sufficient. Maintenance will probably be irregular on such a utility machine, so steel parts should be kept to a minimum (the chainset is the exception to this rule). Wheels which stay true will need to be spoked with either the Continental 36/36 arrangement or 32/40 as on British machines. There is no point in light tyres as most townships sport greasy roads that are treacherous in the rain, and tubes of butyl will hold the air for long spells. This is just about the only bicycle where the weight of a prop stand is justified. If you prefer to buy off the peg, it is just possible that a Moulton will suit, although doubtless before long you would want to replace the saddle and wheels, if not more . . .

If you are looking for a special touring bicycle, then a small wheeled type is also worth consideration. Re-equipped with first class fittings, the Moulton, with its low centre of gravity, would become an excellent carrier for heavy loads. If you intend to tour principally in flat country a massed start bicycle with mudguards and a saddlebag will serve very well. If, however, you intend to spend long hours in the saddle, traverse mountain ranges and perhaps carry camping gear, then a real tourer is something less than a luxury.

In such a machine, 18in chain stays give a little extra comfort and I reduce the bracket height to 10½in. When time is no object there is no need to pedal round corners, so a low bracket is acceptable and this helps one feel part of the bicycle. Because gearing will have to go down to the lower 30s a derailleur which is designed with these wide ratios in mind should be chosen. The Shimano Titlist G.S. or Huret

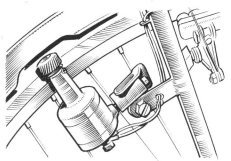

This Lucifer dynamo is bolted to a bracket brazed on the seat stay.

Super Touring gear would be ideal. To obtain these low gears a touring double chainwheel will be necessary (examples will be found in the T.A. range). It is not necessary to have very close ratios and a top gear in the upper 70s should suffice. There is a vogue for triple chainwheels, but these simply increase weight for no very good reason. You may also be tempted to fit a six cog freewheel. With an 18 in chainstay, malalignment of the chain would not be too disastrous, but again there seems to be little point in them. I suggest that five gears on the large chainwheel, with the sixth as an extra low achieved by switching to the small chainwheel, will provide a trouble-free arrangement, and you will not need to carry a computer to decide which ratio to engage and how to select it.

Elsewhere in the book you will find pictures of Randonneur bars, which are worth considering, and brazed-on cantilever brakes. Clips on the frame should be

avoided – rough roads will soon loosen dynamo fittings, for example, as they are attached to tapering tubes. I use a dynamo because I enjoy riding at night but admit that it is a heavy luxury if needed only on the odd occasion.

The camper will certainly need all the space panniers can provide but they do have another advantage, in keeping the load low down. If you intend to use the bicycle for everyday rides it is simple to remove the panniers and rear carrier, leaving a small bag on the handlebars.

The road racing man is in a happier position. Continental manufacturers have always built frames to satisfy his requirements: Britain has followed suit in recent years and in addition has a nucleus of small makers who build frames to delight the connoisseur. In equipping your bicycle there are economies which can be made without sacrificing efficiency. I doubt if there is a bad derailleur on sale today. I would not replace

A modern American lightweight.

ny Campagnolo with any other type, because it has never let me down and is a delight to use, but Huret, Maeda and Shimano, to name but three, should be quite adequate and leave some cash in hand for those components which really will help you to go faster. Likewise the brakes. No one need think he is taking his life in his hands by using an inexpensive pair of side-pulls. The best wheels you can afford, well shod, and driven by a light but rigid alloy chainset will be expensive, but saddle apart, this is the last area in which to economise. It does not cost a cent more to select the best gear ratios, though, and an even spread between 54 and 102 can be obtained with a five sprocket block of 14, 15, 16, 17, and 19, used in conjunction with 38 and 53 tooth chainwheels. Unshipping a chain is a nuisance to a tourist but it is tragic in a race, so if possible avoid the transmission malalignment of six sprocket free-wheels.

The time trial is not common enough outside Britain for many riders to have a special bicycle for the job, and certainly a massed start mount is almost ideal for this purpose. Because the effort is even, and the rider chooses where he rides on the road, lighter wheels and tyres are in order. It is common to dispense with a second chainwheel, and some of the best riders use a single fixed gear, saving the weight of a rear brake. But these are for the dedicated time trial enthusiast. On the Continent such events are usually just single stages in road races. In Britain the selection of flat, well surfaced roads has encouraged the use of special bicycles for time trials.

A form of racing where special equipment is really necessary is cyclo-cross, where the rapid increase in popularity will no doubt lead to the introduction of more and better components. There are plenty of tubulars available with treads specially designed for this type of racing, but for the rest of the machine it is just a case of selecting the lightest components you can get away with. The subtleties of double-chain-wheels are out, and there is no point in ruining a leather saddle, either. In fact the average rider will be tempted to use some old equipment which is past its best anyway. The special T.A. chainring helps keep a chain in place, and pedals with tongues can save valuable seconds in the many remounts of a race.

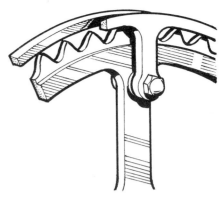

Side plates on this T.A. cyclo-cross chainwheel help to stop derailment.

Although outside the bicycling mainstream, bicycle polo is popular in Britain and America.

Left: A Tour de France time trial stage, where specialists excel—this is the Dutch rider Zoetemells.

Opposite, above: This is a typical track machine. The fixed gear transmission provides the only form of braking. The frame has a shorter wheelbase, and is more upright in design than a road racing bicycle, and as a result is more responsive.

Opposite: Sprinters at a standstill, each waiting for the other to make a move.

You will see by the dimensions in the diagram that a track bicycle has a shorter wheelbase, and is a more upright design than a road machine. It must be rigid and responsive and capable of transmitting violent bursts of energy which would be wasteful in any other branch of the sport. Round section fork blades are used, and wheel clearances are smaller as there is no need to cater for brakes and mudguards. Seat and chain stays are stiffer than on road frames, and the drive they help to transmit comes via a block chain of 1in pitch. This is only necessary in sprinting. The pursuit rider will not need or even want such a drive. The smoothness of a $\frac{3}{32}$in chain has made it increasingly popular here, for as in road time trials, the rider's energy is spread out as evenly as possible.

Track racing is a rather unsociable form of cycling even on tandems, but in their road going state these are often the best answer for a man and wife combination. When the going is tough the husband just has to try a little harder and it is possible to carry on a decent conversation.

If you opt for a tandem, then a sympathetic frame-maker will be

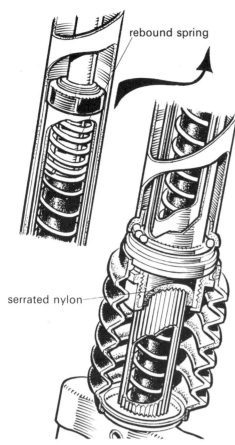

rebound spring

serrated nylon

Front suspension on the Moulton is effected by rubber and a coil spring, with a degree of damping between.

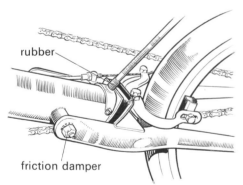

rubber

friction damper

Rear suspension on the Moulton small wheel bicycle.

needed. Some tandem frames have an open design at the rear, known as lady-back. But it is highly desirable that the frame does not whip, so if possible keep to the 'double-gents' style with a through top tube. Track tandems, you will notice, have a curved rear seat tube. This helps to shorten the wheel base, but for touring makes for a rather rough trip for the rear rider. Balloon tyres, once popular on French tandems, do help to absorb the shocks from bad roads, but are a poor solution, and take much of the pleasure out of riding.

Tandem gear ratios will need to be wider than on a single. With a tail wind really high average speeds are possible, for the frontal area is the same as for a conventional machine, but unless the riders are a good match, hills can be tough. It is best to sit and twiddle on slopes you might be tempted to ride up out of your saddle on a single. So an even spread of low gear ratios will help. The success of tandem riding probably lies in having a partner with a similar riding style. If you are not compatible, the best tandem in the world won't help much.

The specialists who make tandem frames have developed ways of adapting equipment to suit, and in most cases should be left to fit what is best, in the most practical manner. Components will be stressed more highly and yet it is necessary in the main to use parts designed for singles. So only the best is good enough.

Bicycle design has not altered significantly for the best part of 100 years, but in the 1960s Alex Moulton, the man who designed the rubber suspension system on the British Mini car, turned his brain in our direction. The result was a 16in wheel bicycle employing rubber to take up road shocks. As the diagrams show, rubber and a spring are employed at the front, providing some damping as the rubber is trapped in the compressing coils. The rear rubber is in both compression and torsion. The Moulton is now made by Raleigh Industries in

three sizes, the two smaller ones using 14in wheels. Ron Kitching of Harrogate has everything you will need to turn a Moulton into a first-class lightweight.

These days, every fashion-conscious child seems to ride a high riser. Raleigh make one of

these too, called the Chopper. As a design it is great fun, and the kids love them, but I'd rather see them on one of these smaller Moulton types. One of the problems with children is that no sooner have you bought them something, than it becomes too small. Well, the Moulton takes care of that, and is safe to ride into the bargain. Unlike some small wheel designs which need balloon tyres to soften the ride, the Moulton has a low rolling resistance which will help to win converts to the sport.

High risers can be great fun for children.

Right, far right and below: This American bicycle factory employs mass-production techniques to a greater extent than European lightweight manufacturers.

Below, right: A typical American amateur road race line-up.

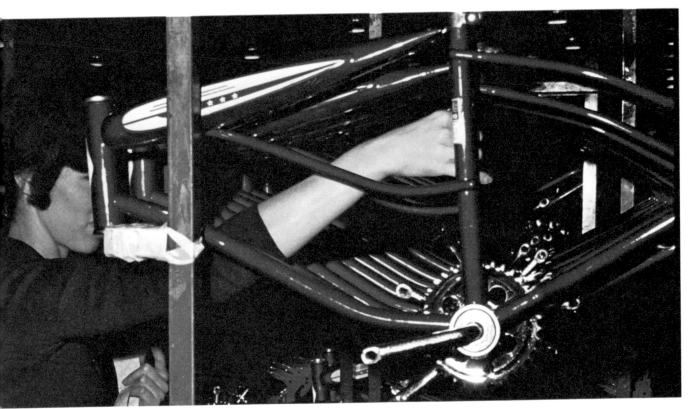

Frames

At some time between 1869 and 1873 the safety bicycle was born. The basic concept is with us still, admittedly in a more sophisticated form, but 100 years is a long time. It has withstood a severe battering by the inventors of this world, and come through unscathed. Nevertheless modern technology has improved methods of construction, and in particular the materials used, to a degree that has made it utterly reliable. I have only suffered one tube failure in many years of riding, and that is about average. When I think of the battering my bicycles have taken on rough tracks, laden with touring equipment, I realise the value of this slow logical development which makes up in refinement what it lacks in sensation.

Effectively there are only two methods of construction: lug brazing and welding. Resin bonded frames have been made experimentally, and we seem to be on the threshold of carbon fibre developments, but these are for the future. By far the most popular type of frame employs lugs into which the tubes are brazed. Welding is cheaper, and in some circumstances where suitable lugs are not available, it is the only way, but it is very much a second best solution.

The lugs used in lightweight frames are made in a variety of designs by Nervex, Bocama, Milremo and other firms–the drawings show some of the former, which are quite typical. The cutaway looks decorative and it saves weight, but it also allows the brazing material to flow into the joint more easily, has some spring which reduces the risk of tube pinching as the joint cools, and

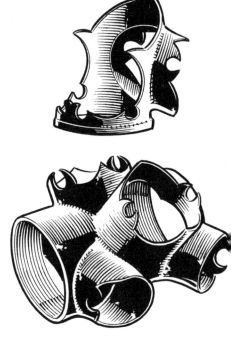

Above: These Nervex lugs are typical of high quality cut-away types.

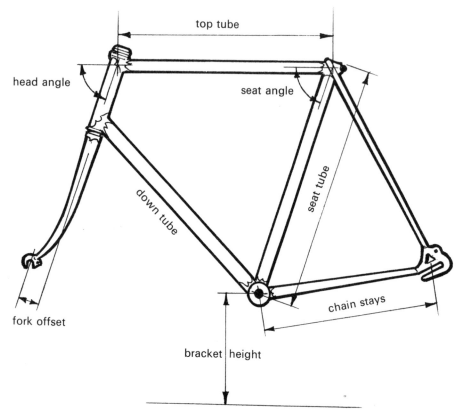

Left: The important frame dimensions are shown on this diagram.

spreads the change of section over a greater length. The tubing used is butted at each end to provide thicker material at the joints. Reynolds 531 is used for most top quality frames from Britain, Columbus and Durifort being its Continental equivalents. Whether the frame is brazed or welded, it must have solid forged fork ends. There are special rear ends for derailleurs made by Simplex and Campagnolo, for example, while Cinelli make a fine track end (a typical selection is illustrated). Fork blades are usually oval for all but track frames, which have round section forks. The fork crown, which does a lot of work, is also a solid forged component. After years with hardly a change we can now fit the elegant new sloping designs by Cinelli, Milremo and Prugnat (shown in the drawing).

In the past many enthusiasts would never have dreamed of just going into a shop and buying a frame. After long deliberations, a bespoke frame-maker would be engaged to cater for personal whims (some of the designs I have heard of have been geometrically impossible, others highly undesirable!) It is still a very nice idea to have a 'personal' frame made, and in the case of people with long legs, it is a necessity. The best approach is to go along to a frame builder and tell him just what you want the bicycle for. He usually knows best. At the same time, if you are going to use certain items like a dynamo, carriers or derailleurs, he can braze on the fittings to carry them. Nasty accidents can result from clips on tapered fork blades coming loose, and quite apart from the aesthetic aspects, I would strongly advise having such items solidly mounted. This is also the time to decide whether you are going to use independent cantilever brakes, because the four bosses will have to be brazed to the fork blades and seat stays.

The frame houses four bearings, bottom bracket and headset. The bottom bracket is the heart of your bicycle, doing an enormous amount of work. If the bearing surfaces start to wear, or dirt and water get in, the result will send the sensitive rider straight into his workshop. Many years ago I prevented this situation with a home-made bottom bracket liner.

The drawing shows what it looks like. Quite a lot of rubbish gets shaken loose from the insides of the tubes, and this device stops it getting into the bearings, while any moisture which finds its way through saddle holes into the stem is also kept at bay. If you decide to fit a liner, it can be cut out of thin aluminium, brass, or even plastic. The bearing has a grease nipple, of course, but I have noticed that the grease tends to get stuck to the axle, where it happily rotates without doing its job. So I use heavy oil instead, which does find its way on to the bearing surfaces.

The bearings which have become universal are of the cup and cone type. Annular and more recently needle roller races have been marketed, but have not proved popular. The right-hand cup is fixed and on British frames a left-hand thread is used. The left-hand cup, which always has a right-hand thread, is adjustable, being secured by a lock ring. When correctly adjusted there should be just a trace of shake at the end of the crank. If the bearing emits a banging noise it is probably nothing worse than water in the races–not much is done to stop rain getting between the axle and cup (the Campagnolo Nuovo Record set has a grooved hole to throw back water). If you get this trouble, just take the unit down, clean and reassemble it.

While the bottom bracket takes heavy loads, and uses a small number of large balls, the converse is true for the head bearings. It is vital that they run absolutely smoothly. The problem is that movement is small, and most of the time the balls are pressing on one part of the track. Road shocks passed up through these bearings will in time tend to cause small indentations, and the steering

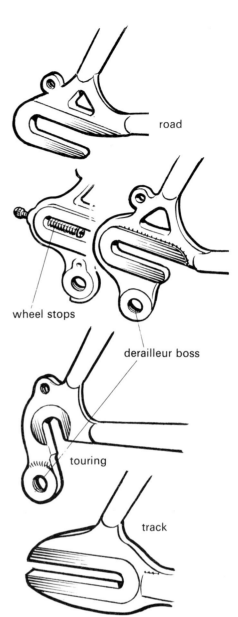

Four typical rear fork ends. Alongside the upper derailleur version is shown Campagnolo's unit with wheel stops.

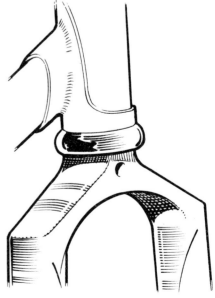

A fashionable sloping fork crown.

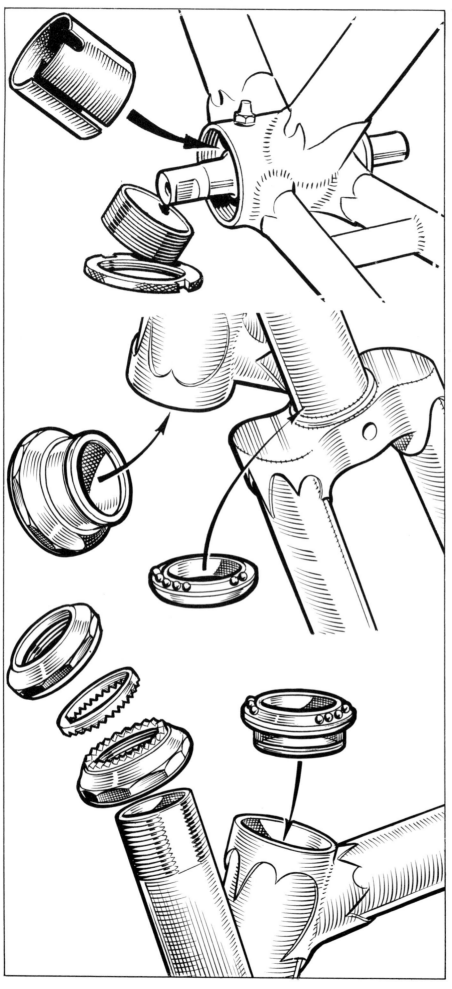

will rotate in a series of jerks. If this happens, throw them away. Wear of this sort and bad adjustment will show up in a simple test-ride without your hands on the bars (but I am not suggesting that you should normally ride along with your hands in your pockets!).

The drawing here shows the type of head bearing almost certainly fitted to your bicycle. Another type, where the top lock ring is used to clamp the handlebar stem, is not so common, but in any case uses similar bearings. The adjustment of these bearings is quite critical. If there is more than a trace of slack the forks will judder when the front brake is applied. If they are too tight then the steering will become positively dangerous. There is rarely any provision for lubrication nowadays, so assemble with grease, or a heavy molybdenum lubricant.

The seat pillar is held in place by a pinch bolt which is sometimes also used to locate a centre-pull rear brake cable hanger. If the frame is the right size for you, then it will not be necessary to expose many inches of pillar. For this reason, there is no need for a steel one. My first bicycle had a frame that was too small and the alloy pillar broke just above the seat tube, so I had an 80-mile ride home with my knees knocking against my chin. This need not happen to you.

Top: This bottom bracket liner will help keep the bearings clean.

Centre: Lower head bearing.

Left: Upper head bearing. The locknut washer is located on a flat on the fork column.

Wheels

Whatever use we put our wheels to, whether it is racing, touring or just carrying home the shopping, the demands on them are considerable. They have to be comfortable yet responsive, run absolutely true, and be light in weight and reliable. So the choice is going to have to be something between a compromise and a keeps to well-surfaced roads and travels light there is no reason why he should not enjoy the lower rotating weight of such wheels.

Most tourists, however, will use wired-on tyres (or clinchers). These will certainly never roll off the rim on bends, can stand more abuse on rough surfaces and are cheaper. There is a weight penalty,

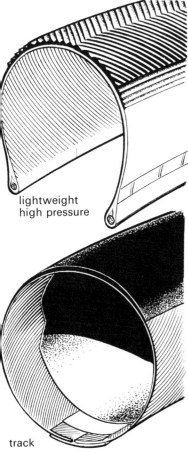

lightweight
high pressure

track

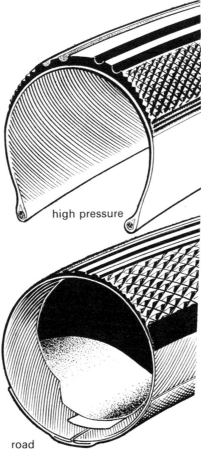

high pressure

road

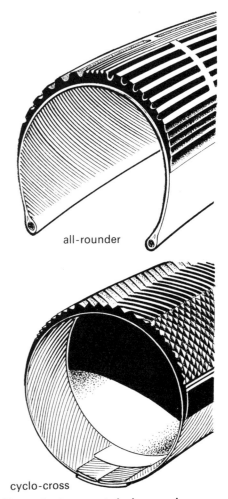

all-rounder

cyclo-cross

Six typical tyres, tubulars and wired-on types.

gamble. If you are a racing man, then tubulars or sew-ups, whichever name you prefer, are ideal. These wheels use covers which completely encase their tubes, and can be quickly peeled off the rim if punctured. They are held on the rim by a combination of air pressure and adhesive. The tourist whose perambulations are more leisurely need not bother about speedy changes, but if he but you will not have to carry spares, although it is not a bad idea to have a spare tube when on vacation. Being a belt and braces man, I also take a short piece of cover to stuff inside any bad gash a tyre might suffer.

Whichever type you decide on, and the size which is almost exclusively used now is 27in, problems don't end there. Hubs come with flanges large or small

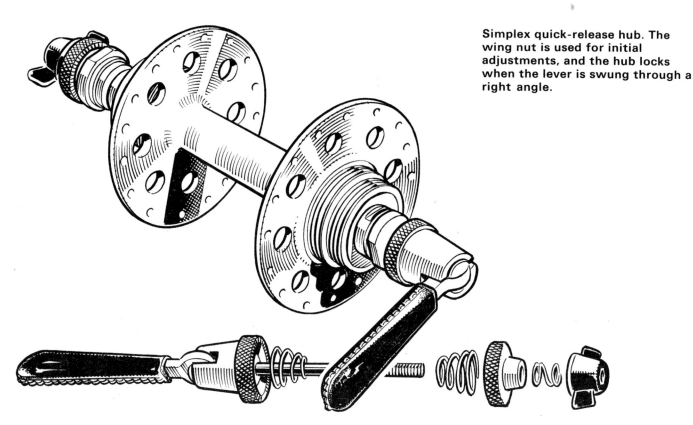

and are secured in various ways.
Wide flange hubs help to make stiff
wheels, together with tying and
soldering of the spokes. Track
riders use track nuts which lack
dangerous projections. Road racing men who need to effect quick
changes after puncturing will use
quick-release hubs, typical of
which are those made by Simplex

and Campagnolo. A drawing
shows the Cinelli Bivalent which
leaves the derailleur system intact
and the hands free of grease
during this unpleasant activity.
Personally I prefer quick-release
hubs even on my wired-on wheels,
but if they are too expensive,
there really is nothing wrong with
a pair of wing nuts.

Wide flange hubs will be usefu
for the tourist who wants a
strong back wheel, while my
feeling is that a small flange fron
wheel helps to cushion the road
shocks a little. By using duralu
min hubs you will not be faced
with the prospect of throwing out
a wheel because the steel barre
has rusted, but there is much to

The Cinelli Bivalent quick-release
system leaves the derailleur intact,
and front and rear wheels are
interchangeable.

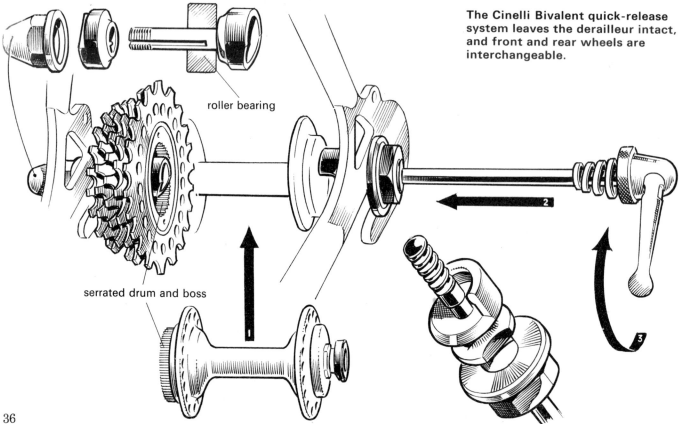

roller bearing

serrated drum and boss

e said for a steel rear hub where fixed gear is used, as there is less hance of a stripped thread. There s a hub which has a derailleur hread on one side and facilities or a fixed cog on the other. Iowever this double-sided hub hould be avoided, because the langes have to be too close ogether, and this makes it im- ossible to build a really strong heel.

Rim design for wired-on tyres as developed from the West- vood type still used with stirrup rakes, through Endricks with heir braking flats on the sides to he narrower high pressure de- igns most common today. These re available in steel, stainless or hromed, and duralumin. The ltra-cautious tourist might hoose a wide based Endrick attern rim for his rear wheel, ut the narrower $1\frac{1}{4}$in rims will uit most riders. I am still using a ery old stainless steel front

wheel, but its original partner has long since given up, for the combination of age hardening and my weight have proved too much for the spoke holes.

Rims for tubulars are hollow and need reinforcement. This is achieved either by eyelet cups for the spokes, riveted between the inner and outer surfaces, or by using wood inserts–or the problem is just ignored. The wood insert solution is to be found in the lightest designs. Here again duralumin is the basic material used and the sides are some- times abraided to assist braking.

Having decided on rims and hubs there is still a small problem. How many spokes? The French and Italians have for many years used 36 spokes front and rear as their standard; the conservative British for years preferred 32 at the front and 40 at the rear. Racing men in their efforts to reduce weight commonly use 28/

32, sometimes 28/28, and now 24 spoke wheels are appearing. The choice will depend not only on the use to which the wheels will be put, but also on personal pedalling capability and weight. There is certainly no sense in a touring man taking a gamble for the sake of a few ounces, and 32/40 or 36/36 would be sensible if he is not intending to carry the kitchen range. A pursuit or time trial rider who moves at an even pace will be able to use light wheels, but the sprinter and road racing man making sudden ex- plosive demands on his bicycle ought to keep to the 36/36 com- bination. Few people will want to spend spare time polishing spokes so the stainless steel type should be used. These are butted or double-butted with the larger diameter at each end or just at the bend. The usual combination is 15/17g, but heavier riders might profit by the 14/16g type. Certainly

Some typical rim sections.

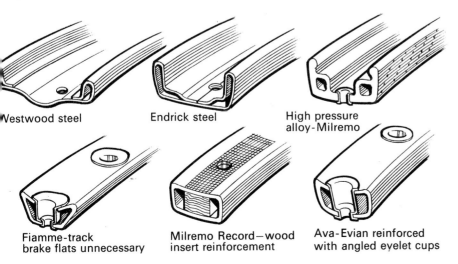

Vestwood steel   Endrick steel   High pressure
                                                alloy-Milremo

Fiamme-track   Milremo Record—wood   Ava-Evian reinforced
brake flats unnecessary insert reinforcement   with angled eyelet cups

I would always choose the heavier spokes for the rear wheel where loads are to be carried.

The choice of tyres for racing is wide, and each manufacturer offers a range which covers the demands of sprinters, pursuit riders, grass track and massed start men, while there are special designs for cyclo-cross riding and time trials. Tubulars come in weights from 13oz (training tyre) to $4\frac{1}{4}$oz, which are hand-made silks for cement track work. The makers even produce these very light designs with different tread patterns for each wheel. The massed start rider, who needs to corner on different surfaces, needs more strength in the side walls, whilst a time trial gives the rider some choice of the line he takes on the road, so he can often get away with a pursuit man's tyre. Whatever the choice it is as well to try to follow the manufacturer's selection, and if possible buy tyres several months before you need to use them. This will give the rubber a chance to mature.

Wired-on tyres are not so highly strung as tubular tyres, so the range of designs is more restricted. Basically there are heavies with knobbly treads, safe under most conditions, and agony to ride. You might need one on the back of a tandem, a bicycle with heavily laden panniers, or on snow and ice. A medium grade type with parallel tread is the maid of all work, whilst there are high pressure lightweight tyres, some as responsive as tubulars, which are a joy to ride. Users of these wired-on tyres at least have a choice of inner tube. If you dislike the daily chore of topping up the pressure, try butyl tubes. They are heavier but do hold their pressure over long periods. Most tubes use high pressure valves, and the drawing shows that the valve is screwed up on its seating when inflation is completed.

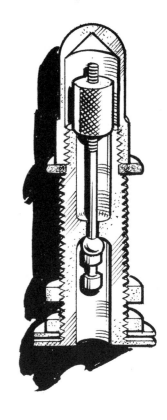

High pressure valve. The locking nut pulls the valve on to its seating

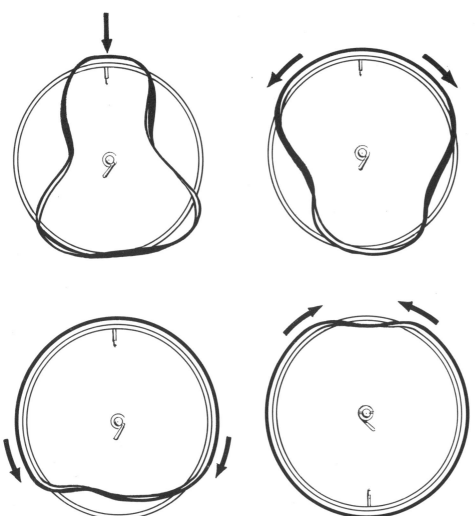

When fitting a tubular, start at the valve, then work round evenly each side.

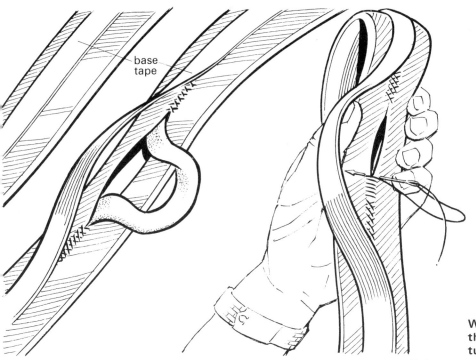

base
tape

When stitching up a tubular, pinch the walls in to avoid damaging the tube.

Fitting these tyres should be easy and although some are a tight fit when new, it should not be necessary to use tyre levers. First check the rim for protruding spokes, and file any offenders flush. Then fit a rim tape. One wire of the cover should now be slid on to the rim. Put a few pumps of air in the tube, place the valve in its hole and feed the tube in. The air should help it to go into place without wrinkles. Leave a trace of air in the tube and ease the other wire on to the rim. The last few inches will be tough going so work round the cover, easing it to ensure that it is seating correctly. Once it is on put a couple more pumps of air in the tube, and go round the cover easing it from side to side to make certain the tube is not pinched anywhere. Inflate to the desired pressure – two pumps before it blows up! – and screw down the valve nut. Pressures in other tyres are not so critical as in tubulars and frankly I go on pumping until my thumb can just push the wall in $\frac{1}{8}$in or so. The lighter the cover, though, the more air it will need. The only time I have enjoyed riding soft wired-on tyres was when wet snow was falling after dark on a cambered ice-covered road.

When you have the misfortune to puncture one of these tyres, it will most likely be in conditions like this, when a spare tube will ease the blood pressure. When removing the cover use those tyre levers carefully. There is not so much rubber and fabric around the wires that they can stand a lot of abuse. When you have found the hole, don't just mend it, but have a look at the cover, remove the offending flint, and if necessary solution some canvas inside to mend the gash. Some French chalk spread around the patches will stop them sticking in the wrong places.

When it comes to fitting tubulars it is as well to remember that they can easily roll off on bends if this job is not done properly. After cleaning the rim, apply several coats of the right cement. There are two basic types, one for track use and the other for road work. To make things easier Vittoria market a universal cement and it only needs one coat. Mastice Gutta is a road tyre cement, whilst Gomme Lacca is for track work. Apply a coat of rim cement to the tubular's base tape, and leave it until it is tacky. If by any chance this base tape has become worn it is a good idea to fit a new tape to the rim, cementing both sides. When fitting the tyre first secure the valve and pull the two sides on evenly, making sure that it has

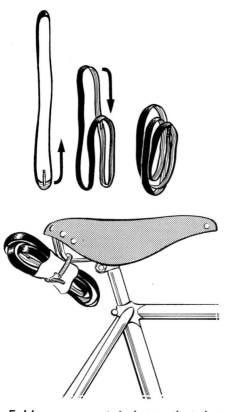

Fold your spare tubular so that the tread is always on the outside, keeping the valve at a bend.

The ball cups on this alloy hub are inserts and the locknut washer is located on a grooved spindle to stop it rotating.

not moved out of line. Before inflating hard, pump the tyre up softly and work round it to ensure that it is seating squarely. Pressures for tubulars are much higher than for clinchers, and the heavier ones need less air. Pirelli recommend 57-71psi for their range, but this is much lower than some riders use. Weight, and the conditions where the tyres are to be used, will affect the issue. Some track tyres will take up to 150psi whilst most massed start riders will use 90-110psi.

Repairing these tyres can be left to professionals if you can locate one. But if you choose to repair your own or just have to do the job yourself, the drill is to first locate the puncture. This is easier when the tyre is still on the wheel for when it is un-supported the air can more easily escape from the cover elsewhere. So immerse the tyre section by section in water until a stream of bubbles appears. Dry the cover, remove the rim, and pull up the base tape for a few inches. Now cut a short section of stitching and and pull out some four or five inches of tubing. You can put some air in it to locate the hole precisely, repeating the water treatment if necessary (try to keep the carcase dry though). Roughen the area around the hole as you would do with a

wired-on tyre, apply solution and use a thin patch, if possible from a repair kit made for tubulars. Vittoria, for example, make the adhesives mentioned earlier, and market everything needed for surgery. Chalk the repair, replace the tube, apply some air to straighten it and sew up the cover. Probably few people can emulate the original stitching but a simple blanket style will do. Now re-stick the base tape. In-flate the tyre and if needed fill the flint hole in the tread with stopping compound. The job does not take too long if one has a proper repair kit; the stitching sounds formidable but is eased if the existing holes are used as shown in the sketches.

When racing it is usually necessary to carry a spare or or even two. Tubulars can easily be folded with the tread on the outside, and the valve at a bend, to reduce chafing, as shown in the sketch. Do not leave them folded longer than necessary. Tourists who use tubulars might carry some rolls of double-sided tape to use instead of cement when changing tyres out in the wilds, if at all doubtful about the quality of the joint.

Well made wheels usually give little trouble, but on tour it is as well to have a few spare spokes. When fitting one remember the bend, *not* the head, rests in the counter-sunk side of the hole. The wheel bearings will occas-ionally need adjustment, and after loosening the lock nut, adjust the cone so that there is a barely perceptible shake with the lock nut re-tightened. Some hubs have grease nipples which are fine, for dirt gets forced out, but racing hubs usually need assembling with grease, or light oil for track riding. One of the moly lubri-cants can be used to reduce drag even more. Quick-release hubs are adjusted on the frame by lightly screwing up the adjuster on the opposite side to the locking lever. Trial and error will produce the desired result and it should not be necessary to heave the lever round to lock the wheel.

Gears

The first pedal-driven bicycles did not have the luxury of gearing, let alone a choice of ratios. The largest gear a rider could push depended on the length of his leg, hence the large driving wheel on ordinary machines. The method by which gear ratios* are still calculated recalls those days, for the final figure represents the diameter of a wheel, the circumference of which would be the distance travelled for one revolution of the pedals. For example, the most popular ratio for riding is obtained by using 27in wheels with a 48-tooth chainwheel and an 18-tooth sprocket; 27 multiplied by 48, divided by 18 gives us 72. The Continentals logically take the calculation a step farther and give the circumference in metres. The 72in gear which has a circumference of 226in becomes 5.60 metres.

The most basic form of transmission is a single fixed gear, driven by a chain of $\frac{1}{2}$in pitch. Apart from the 1in block chains used on the track for sprinting, all the three major types are of this pitch. Heavy and trade bicycles usually employ $\frac{3}{16}$in chains; single drives and hub gears use $\frac{1}{8}$in chains, and derailleurs have a special flexible $\frac{3}{32}$in size. This last type is often used to drive a single fixed gear, too.

This simple transmission can be a delight to ride. I can remember riding from London to York on Good Friday with the North Road Cycling Club annual event, and touring the Yorkshire Dales during Easter, when most of us were happily using such drives. In these days of 18-speed transmissions it may seem odd, but it did teach us how to pedal.

The sketch shows how the sprocket is locked in place by a ring using a left-hand thread. Hubs designed for single gears have threads on either side of the wheel. In the days before derailleurs, riders would hastily turn their wheels round before beginning a steep climb, and use a bigger sprocket on the other side. A single freewheel will fit this type of hub.

One of the advantages of a single fixed gear becomes obvious when riding through traffic, or in company. A slight back pressure on the pedals is enough to slow you down gently, and gives a greater feeling of confidence when riding at slow speed.

When fitting a single gear, use the standard bottom bracket axle to achieve a straight chain line. If a chain spring connecting link is fitted, remember that its closed end must face in the direction of chain travel. With the wheel nuts tightened there should be $\frac{1}{2}-\frac{3}{4}$in of slack on the lower run of the chain. If everything was perfect this could be reduced a little, but chainwheels are not always quite true, and a cottered crank which is not a tight fit on its axle will be driven slightly out of centre when the cotter is inserted.

When it is necessary to remove a sprocket, first undo the locking ring clockwise with a 'C' spanner, then wrap the chain of a sprocket removing tool round the teeth and turn anti-clockwise with the end of the bar firmly resting between two teeth. On no account try to knock it off, for the teeth are easily damaged.

Sooner or later a chain will wear out, and this manifests itself in two ways. There will be a slight crunchy feeling to the drive, and when you push the chain at the front of the chainwheel it will appear to have

A 'C' spanner and sprocket removing tool, needed to dismantle a fixed gear.

*A gear table appears on page 95

stretched. What actually happens is that the rivet holes and pins wear, and the pitch becomes slightly more than ½ in. The rear sprocket is the next item to wear, and the chainwheel last. Keeping the system as free from grit as possible will help to prolong life, and when lubricating just drip oil on to the inside of the chain, wiping off any excess.

Of the many hub gears that were once available, Sturmey Archer seems to be the only

tres on a three-speed wide ratio unit. It has an upward shift from normal of 33.3 per cent, and a downward shift of 28.6 per cent. This unit can be bought on its own, or with a back-pedalling brake, a hub brake, or a dynohub. The normal gear depends of course on the selection of chainwheel and rear sprocket. There is also an automatic two-speed hub which changes on a backward kick of the pedals. It gives normal, and 28.6 per cent down ratios. The

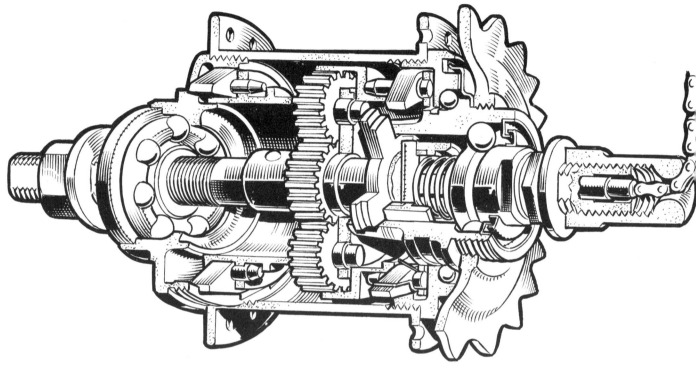

survivor. For many there are distinct advantages to be had from their use. Ease of adjustment and lack of maintenance endear them to the non-enthusiast. Most complaints about this type centre around the widely spaced ratios that are imposed by the epicyclic system. Driving through a system of gears will of course involve losses, and the hubs are not light. I have used one of the discontinued close ratio hub gears in hilly races, and am convinced that gear shifting was slower than with a derailleur. Despite these disadvantages (lack of choice in selecting ratios being the worst), I notice that my club's 24-hour race has been won year after year by the only man in the event with such a gear.

The range produced now cen-

five-speed hub provides ratios of 50 per cent and 26.6 per cent above normal, and 21.1 per cent, then 33.3 per cent below. Sadly the days of the medium and close ratio hubs are gone.

The illustration shows the basic three-speed version. When top gear is selected the sprocket drives the planet cage. The sun gear on the spindle is a fixture, and the planet pinions rotating around it drive the outer gear ring faster. This passes the drive through the right hand pawls to the wheel. In bottom gear the sprocket drives this outer gear ring, which forces the planet cage to rotate. The reduced drive is passed to the wheel by the left hand set of pawls. The set on the right are retracted by the sliding clutch, but when top gear is used

The Sturmey Archer three-speed hub (shown here in middle gear).

the left hand pawls are over-ridden, hence the ticking noise. The five-speed hub works on the same principle, but needs two gear trains to achieve its ends.

Adjusting a hub gear is important as it must be absolutely accurate. Fortunately this is not too difficult. The diagram shows that both the three- and five-speed hubs have a similar arrangement on the right hand side. Set the three-speed in its number two position, the five-speed in its central position. The change of section from round to flat on the control rod should line up with the end of the spindle. If it does not, then undo the adjuster locking nut, turn the knurled barrel until it is in line, and re-lock it. The five-speed version has a similar adjuster on the left hand side, operated by bellcrank instead of chain. Set both control levers in their forward positions, and loosen the adjuster locknut. While pulling the left hand control lever back, move the cranks backwards and forwards with the rear wheel stationary. When the mechanism is fully engaged it will be possible to feel the drive via the pedals. Now pull out the bell crank and take up any slack on the adjuster. Re-lock the screw, and check that all is in order by looking through the hole in the side of the bellcrank. The red band on the pushrod should be almost hidden inside the hub spindle. The unit should only need a few drops of oil every month, and this should be of a light grade. Should you wish to change the sprocket, this entails removing a circlip and washer. The sprocket then slides off.

The derailleur system is now the favourite type of gear, and we tend to think of it as something new, which has taken the place of hub gears. In fact they both came on the scene at roughly the same time. The Linley and Biggs derailleur was patented in 1894, so designers have had plenty of time to think about it. The idea of bending a chain out of line so that it rides up and over its teeth on to the next sprocket still horrifies

some engineers. In my opinion the breakthrough came when narrow $\frac{3}{32}$ in chains designed specifically for this purpose appeared. Before this the $\frac{1}{8}$ in chain was used. When new and stiff, there was a real risk of it running off the top of the chainwheel, and before double jockey cages were introduced chain slip was quite common. It is now possible for a bicycle to be equipped with any set of ratios, and if fitted properly the system will work reliably.

Rear derailleurs not only guide the chain from one sprocket to the next on a cluster of 4, 5, or 6 ratios, but also tension the chain. The front derailleur is basically just a guide mounted on top of the chainwheels which selects one of two or three different sizes. The most popular arrangement consists of a rear derailleur of five sprockets worked in conjunction with two chainwheels. It is certainly possible to use six speed freewheels and triple chainwheels, although it is difficult to see any real justification for this. It is important that the racing man can make subtle changes to suit different conditions, and a ten-speed transmission does this very nicely. The tourist will also want a cluster of gears with quite narrow gaps above and below normal. When you start selecting gears in the 40s, and even lower, these subtleties are lost. Chain malalignment on the extreme combinations is asking rather a lot, and if you seek long life and reliability rather than owning the mostest, I would try to rub along with ten speeds.

There is quite a choice when it comes to selecting the right model. The smoothest way of moving the cage is by means of a swinging parallelogram, which has completely taken over from sliding cages. Adjustment is now simplicity itself and in most cases the two spring-loaded set screws can be positioned to suit four, five or six sprocket freewheels. If you must use the latter, check before buying because in some cases equipment at the cheaper end of the range will only accom-

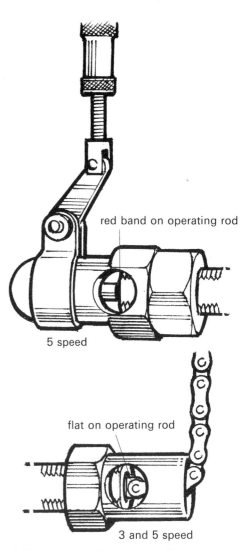

red band on operating rod

5 speed

flat on operating rod

3 and 5 speed

Adjustment indicators on Sturmey Archer gears.

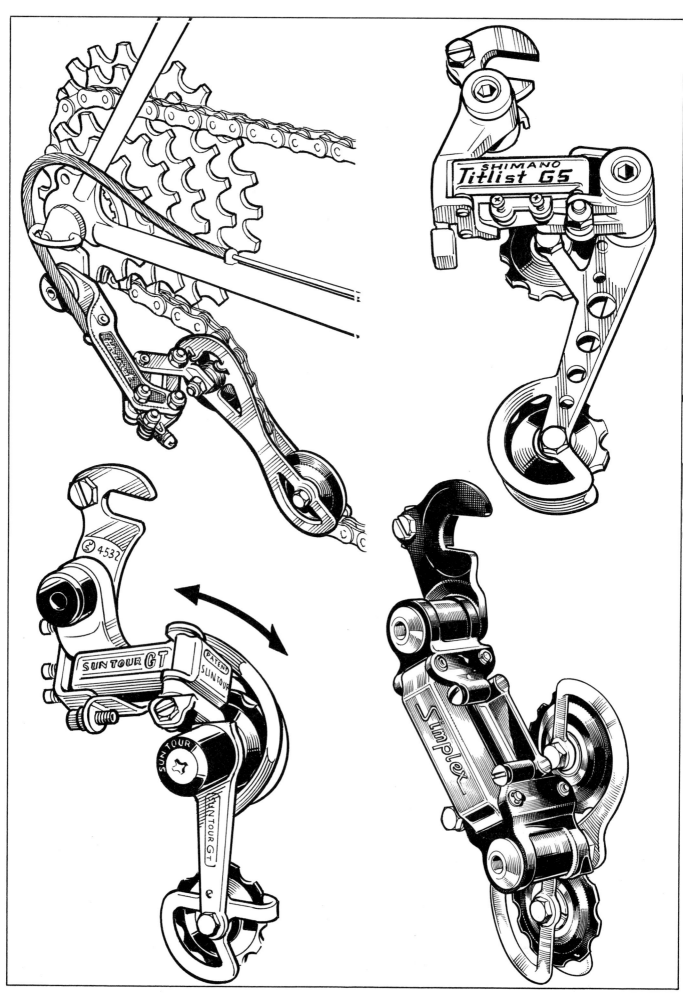

modate five speeds (the Huret Allvit is an example). If you are going to use an extreme range of ratios, then your choice must be among the touring derailleurs. The Huret Super Touring, which is a good example, is based on the company's Competition model, but with a longer cage to take up the extra slack. On the other hand, Campagnolo, who produce as good a racing gear as you could ask for in their Nuovo Record, have a completely separate design in their Gran Turismo mechanism. Both the swinging arms and the jockey cage are tensioned, and their gear certainly has more capacity than any others available. A fore and aft spring on the parallelogram to assist chain tensioning is also used on the Simplex Prestige, Shimano Titlist G.S. and Crane. The Maeda Sun Tour G.T., like the Huret Super Touring, relies on a long jockey cage to take up the chain, and it also does the job well. A feature

of this gear is the angled parallelogram which can be seen in the sketch. This follows the line of the sprocket block, and is an advantage in this design where the top jockey is mounted on the same centre as the cage pivot.

Racing gears which do not have to span such wide ranges are more compact, but of these the Simplex Prestige is capable of meeting the range demanded by less ambitious tourists. It is an interesting design and, in common with its 'professional' stablemate, the Criterium, utilises a plastic called Delrin for much of its construction. This of course reduces the risk of corrosion, but quite frankly, with all the oil that is usually flying around, that is not the main worry. It does make for lightness, which is a definite advantage, but cannot take the knocks that a steel mechanism will withstand.

All the modern derailleurs work well, and it must be up to

you to decide how long you want yours to last, or how much abuse you expect it to take. There is such a thing as brand loyalty, and my old Campagnolo Record has yet to let me down. However, Campagnolo equipment is rather expensive, and the mechanically similar Spanish Zeus Criterium is a good deal cheaper. This gear utilises nylon rollers as does the Huret Competition, another changer like the Cyclo Benelux P.2 that is not outrageously expensive. The choice does seem perplexing. Undoubtedly the high priced Campagnolos are good value if you are still going to be riding in ten years' time.

It is true that some mechanisms will not stand much abuse, but if that was the criteria applied throughout cycle design there would not be a lightweight on the road. I cannot remember ever knocking a gear, so concentrate on selecting a design that will not wear out easily.

Opposite page, top left: The Huret Super derailleur. Top right: The Shimano Titlist G.S. touring derailleur. Lower left: The Maeda Sun Tour derailleur has its parallelogram set at an angle so that the cage follows the angle of the sprocket block. Lower right: The Simplex Prestige derailleur utilises Delrin plastic for the principal parts.

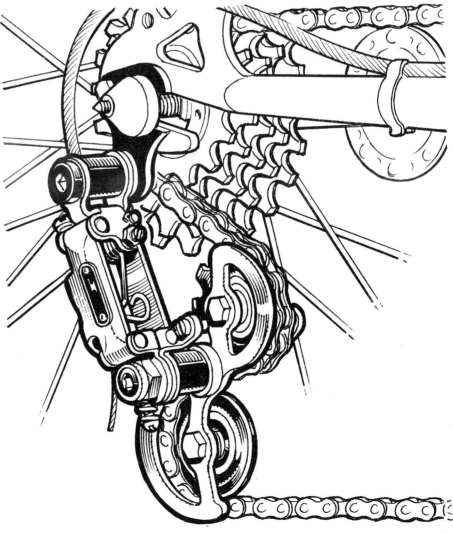

Right: Cyclo Benelux P.2 derailleur.

Left: This Simplex competition front derailleur needs no cables to control it. Right: The Simplex Criterium front changer is of the parallelogram type.

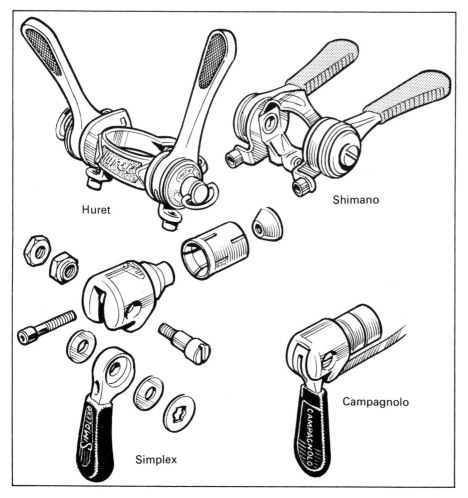

Four gear levers. The lower pair are for handlebar mounting.

Huret

Shimano

Simplex

Campagnolo

Front derailleurs, or changers as they are often called, are available to match the rear mechanisms. There is no technical reason why you should use a matched pair, except that it will look better. Your reasons for buying a particular make will probably apply to the front changer too. With the exception of the Simplex Competition, all are cable operated. The parallelogram principle again makes for the smoothest change. The push rod type work well enough when clean, and on a racing cycle continual use helps, but if neglected or allowed to become clogged with gritty grease, it will let you down. Simplex make a Delrin plastic push rod version for their Prestige gear, but the Criterium sports a swinging front unit, and similar variations apply to the Campagnolo range. Both Huret units work on the parallelogram idea, but the Luxe has a greater range than the Svelto, making it a preferable choice for tourists.

The usual way of shifting gears is through levers, which should be mounted on the down tube. Single or double assemblies are made; Prestige levers are of Delrin, while some of the metal ones, Sun and Crane, for instance, have plastic sleeves. A facility worth looking for is a thumbscrew which will enable you to adjust a slipping lever while on the move. If you find that the lever is too highly geared, and the chain moves two places instead of one, the Simplex device illustrated might help; it comprises a lever pivoted on a clamp, the output side having a shorter movement than the input.

Gear changing certainly takes a little mastering and the secret is to keep up the revs while reducing the pedal pressure. This is asking a lot when ascending a steep hill. Changing down is more difficult for just about every reason, but this is the over-riding one.

You will soon get to know the demands of your particular mechanism. With some it pays to move the lever a little too far, then back,

but so little that at first you are certain to overdo it. My old Campagnolo changes so smoothly that I sometimes commit the unpardonable crime of looking down to make sure it has worked! An alternative to down tube mounted levers is the Simplex or Campagnolo handlebar version. The operating cable is bound under the handlebar tape and runs down in its shroud to a stop on the down tube at just about the point where a lever would normally be fitted. Friction adjusting wing nuts are not practicable with this type of control, and it is advisable to fit rubber sleeves to the projecting levers.

When fitting a derailleur system, malalignment of the chain is unavoidable, but can be kept to a minimum by using the correct bottom bracket axle. The diagram shows that the third sprocket on a five-speed block must be in line with the gap between double chainwheels (there is a correct axle to use for single, double and triple chainsets). When fitting the chain, ensure that there is enough length for it to run not only on the biggest sprocket and chainring, but also to be able to climb over on to the next ratio. This adjustment must be carried out with the wheel in its correct place in the drop-out.

Derailleur chains do not use spring links, and the sort of rivet extractor shown will make the job of chain adjustment easier. When using it, try not to remove the rivet completely; leave it hanging in the far plate. The same tool can be used to push the rivet back in again. The result of this operation will not only be a shorter chain–there will almost certainly be a stiff link which will not run smoothly round the jockeys. So when riveting up the link, waggle it from side to side to loosen the joint a little. If one of these tools is not available, a hammer and punch, or even a nail, will do the job.

Maintenance will consist of regularly removing the grit and stale oil from the mechanism and chain. The rollers are the first to

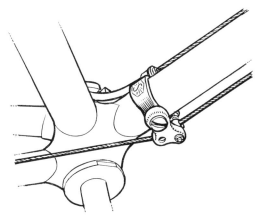

The Simplex Demultiplicator Relais reduces cable movement at the derailleur.

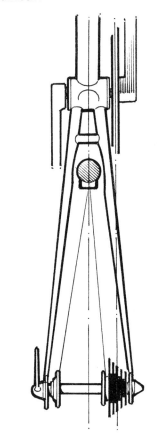

To ensure minimum chain wear, check that the chainwheel is in line with the freewheel unit.

Fifon rivet extractor.

A boss type freewheel, with a typical extractor tool.

Milremo Alpine freewheel and its removing tool.

On this flush-back freewheel the two largest sprockets have left-hand threads.

suffer for their bearings are rather exposed–in extreme cases of neglect a roller just stops rotating. Those which have no teeth or indentations of any sort are the first offenders. Naturally chain wear is more rapid with a derailleur, and when a new chain has been fitted it may not mate too well with the more commonly used sprockets. It may bed in if the trouble is only slight, but it is advisable to renew them at the same time.

Freewheel sprocket blocks have always been a problem. For years no manufacturers bothered to make it easy to remove them from the hub, and this problem still exists, for the fashion of incorporating two slots in the central body dies hard. With a block of this type do not get out the cold chisel. Feed the removing tool over the spindle and tighten a track nut on it. Now lock the tool in a vice, and give a sharp pull on the rim. As soon as the block moves loosen the remover a little, because the freewheel will be pressing harder on it. Better still, buy a unit like the Milremo illustrated. One type of block has a flush back, the other has a boss and it is usual for the sprockets to screw on to the body. The flush back block has its largest sprockets attached by a left-hand thread, while the boss type uses a right-hand thread

throughout. Most hubs are designed for use with flush back units. There are also units like the Milremo Alpine, where the screwed outer sprocket holds in place the larger ratios, which slide on to a series of flats. Lubrication should only be with a thin oil or the pawls might get gummed up. When screwing a unit on to the hub, a smear of oil on the thread will make it easier to remove when the time comes. Most freewheel units cover a range between 13- and 30-tooth sprockets.

Chainsets are made in either steel or light alloy. The former are attached to the bottom bracket axle with cotter pins. A variety of methods have been tried for securing cotterless cranks, but at the moment the most popular method is the slightly tapered square section axle, with the crank pulled up on to the flats by a bolt screwing into it. This arrangement is favoured by Stronglight, Campagnolo and Zeus. T.A. have gone their own way, and the result allows a worthwhile lateral adjustment of 4mm. Another advantage of this method is that an expensive extractor tool is not necessary (it is no great hardship to carry the hexagonal key about).

One of these lightweight sets is the obvious choice for a weight conscious rider, and they have the added advantage of great rigidity

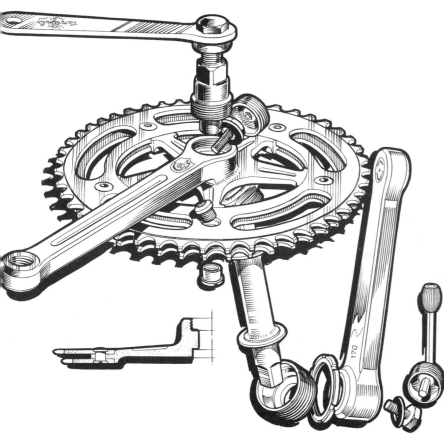

Campagnolo cotterless chainset together with its tools.

Steel chains seem to like running on alloy rings, and the wear rate on them is low. If a set of steel cranks is selected there is, however, no reason why alloy chainrings should not be used. Basically these rings have either a five- or three-pin fixing, and the majority are interchangeable.

Fitting a pair of cottered cranks calls for a little handwork and the aim should be to get a combination of crank and axle with as little clearance as possible. Fit the cotter pin so that the threaded end trails behind as you pedal. Probably the pin will not go in far enough and its flat will have to be filed down bit by bit until there is enough thread through for the nut and washer (try not to leave any transverse file marks when doing this). When knocking a

cotter home, or later on removing it, be sure to support the crank opposite the blow. Failure to do this will result in some nasty damage to the bottom bracket bearings. When knocking a cotter out, a piece of wood or soft metal interposed between the threaded end, from which the nut has been removed, and the hammer, will prevent damage to the thread. If you lack the confidence to do this just loosen the nut and after the cotter is freed unscrewing the nut will take out any slight dents you have made in the thread.

Creaking and grinding noises drive one to despair and can take all the pleasure out of riding—the trouble taken to see that the transmission is working correctly will be well rewarded.

Below, left: T.A. Cotterless cranks.

Below: Always support the crank when knocking out a cotter pin, and fit it so that its head leads when pedalling.

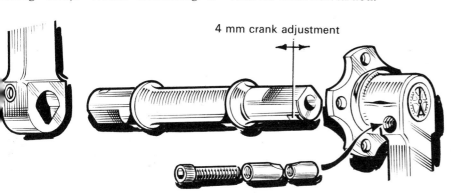

4 mm crank adjustment

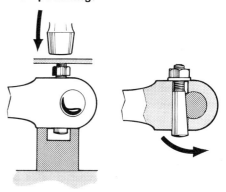

Brakes

There was a time when this would have been a rather painful chapter to write – I recall agonising moments waiting for my brakes to bite, their appalling inefficiency in the wet, and the hours spent coaxing them to work smoothly. Happily the scene has changed dramatically over the last few years with modern alloys and brake block design and the wide choice of different types. Brakes are so good these days that it is as well to remember that it is the tyre tread design which will determine the rate at which you will be able to stop.

There are various ways of bringing a bicycle to a halt. One of the most satisfying methods, and certainly the most reliable, is the fixed wheel. On the track it is the only form of braking, but a machine fitted with a single fixed cog, and at least one rim brake, and that on the front, will be a very safe steed for riding in town where subtle variations in speed are often desirable to keep in the flow of traffic.

Brakes which are applied at the rim are in the majority today. In gripping the rim, less load is placed on the spoking and although there is a drop in efficiency in the rain this in fact is no bad thing for it obviates, or at least reduces, the possibility of a skid developing. Roller lever, or stirrup brakes, whichever one likes to call them, are fitted to the old kind of upright roadster bicycles, and these pull up on the inner face of Westwood rims. The types we should be concerned with, operate on the side faces, and it probably has not escaped your notice that the best automobiles follow suit with their disc brakes. These types can be divided into side-pull and centre-pull.

Side-pull brakes are simple in design and cheaper to buy than any other type. The only disadvantage is the possibility of a slightly uneven braking action. The cable pulls on the calipers at one side of the central pivot, and if there is any stickiness in this pivot one block can sometimes drag on the rim after the lever has been released. This can usually be overcome by adjustment, but no fiddling will quite achieve the delightful smoothness of a centre-pull. Having said that, I must own up to the fact that one of my bikes has Weinmann side-pull brakes that have been completely trouble-free for many years. Campagnolo make this type of brake with their usual standards of workmanship. One make of this type which has perhaps the best of both worlds is the G.B. Synchron, which has the usual cable action at one side but employs two pivots and a self-centring action. It is still possible to buy side-pull brakes made in steel and surprisingly these are no heavier than alloy types, but I would not recommend them. The use of alloy gives greater rigidity while the depth of section allows a firmer pivot; these factors ensure that the blocks are held at the correct angle, and do not spring up in an arc when applied.

The principal virtue of centre-pull brakes is a smooth action. They can be divided into two categories, for although most bolt on the frame in the same way as side-pull types, there is an exception. Mafac or C.L.B. produce brakes under the names of Criterium and Cantil-Racer, which pivot on bosses brazed to the frame. Because the operating levers pivot directly on to the frame, there is absolutely no

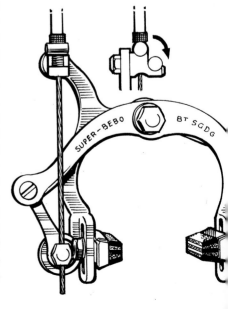

This Beborex side-pull brake has a leverage amplifier incorporated. The quick-release device is shown in detail.

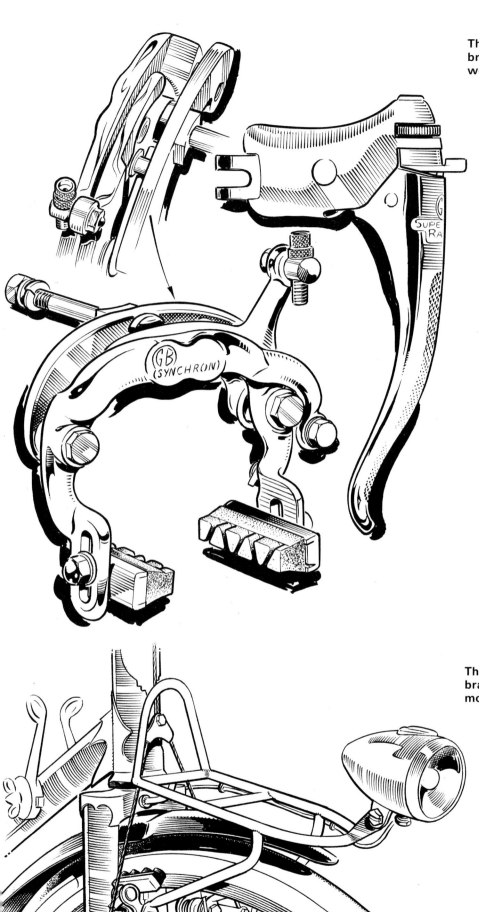

The G.B. Synchron, like a side-pull brake, needs no cable hangers, but works as smoothly as a centre-pull.

These Mafac Criterium centre-pull brakes are used as the lower mounting points for a front carrier.

The Pouliquen brake block is an idea by Milremo. It has a degree of articulation, so is always in line with the rim.

Weinmann cable hangers for centre-pull brakes, with quick-release cams.

chance of whip, and these brakes give one great confidence when descending steep hills laden with touring gear.

In the past when rim brakes were not as efficient as they are today, hub brakes were quite popular. Being enclosed, their efficiency was not reduced by rain, and prolonged application, which generates heat, was kept well away from the tyres. Because the braking action has to be transferred through the spokes it was necessary for these to be of a heavier gauge. But this is all history for most of us. The utility cyclist might possibly want this type, among enthusiasts only tricyclists and tandem riders need show any interest. The usual hub brake employs two expanding shoes and a rear one can be supplied by Sturmey-Archer fitted into a three-speed hub. The other rear brake is of course the coaster. Here the unit is operated by pedalling backwards, so no lever control is needed.

One good reason why brakes are so efficient today lies in the design of the blocks. These no longer just consist of hunks of rubber of a desirable texture for steel or alloy rims, but are carefully shaped so that rain will flow away and at the same time the slight flexibility of the studs gives a better bite. Until recently blocks have been held rigidly to the brake arms, but Milremo have a clever articulated block called the Pou-

liquen which really does ensure perfect contact with the rim. Sometimes one finds when fitting new brakes that the blocks are not quite parallel and these devices would certainly help in this respect. Moreover, the manufacturers claim that their wear rate is lower, that they give better braking in wet weather and are quieter. Because they are not held in shoes as other types are there is no fear of them being knocked out during hasty wheel removal – which brings us to the subject of quick-release devices.

When a brake is adjusted properly the blocks will be too close to the rim to allow an inflated tyre to pass. So some method of speedily increasing the gap is desirable, particularly to the racing man. Some centre-pull brakes have a cam and slot device between the operating and straddle wires. The Mafac Racer uses the straddle wire itself, which is simply unhooked to widen the gap. Weinmann incorporate the cam devices in their frame mounted cable hangers. The version which has most appeal to racing men, though, is that which is built into the lever. There are several types to choose from. The Balila, for example, incorporates a button which is depressed to release the brake. In the heat of a race it is all too easy to forget to reset the tension but here the first application of the lever does this automatically. With the de-

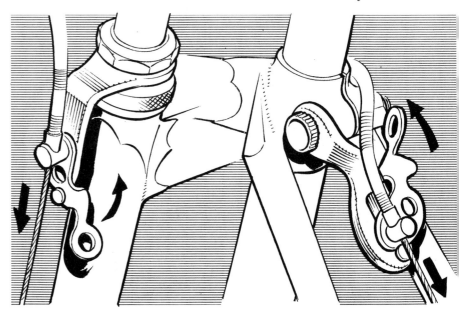

52

vices incorporated in the brake itself it may not be easy to reset when riding, and in any case it may be too late when you find out. Ease of wheel removal is not the only advantage of a quick-release mechanism. In the event of a spoke breaking a wheel may distort so that the rim rubs against the brake blocks. This can be temporarily cured by releasing the mechanism, although one should be careful to see that the greater clearance does not detract too much from braking efficiency.

The thoughtful rider will use his brakes as little as possible–there is after all no point in wasting energy. But however rarely you pull on those brake levers they will be of constant use whilst just riding along. If fitted at the correct angle, and with a rubber hood like the Weinmann version illustrated, they will provide an ideal rest for the hands. Most levers incorporate screwed adjusters, although these are really of little importance–I have never needed to adjust a brake whilst riding. Tourists who use the Randonneur bars will probably want a different shape of lever, which follows the contour of these comfortable bends. Mafac, C.L.B. and Beborex all make suitable ones.

Now comes the problem of deciding which type of brake to fit. All well-made brakes are reliable if fitted correctly, but because they are basically more simple, and have fewer cables to wear, the side-pull type is likely to be the better choice for general use, where maintenance is likely to be minimal. There is also the question of cost–with the exception mentioned earlier, these brakes will certainly be easier on the pocket. They could prove to be a few ounces lighter as well. The centre-pull looks good, and that is enough reason for some riders to buy them, others just buy the best anyway and it does help to know that you are equipped to decelerate in the most refined way! The tourist who has the forethought to order a bespoke frame can gain a positive advantage because by specifying brazed on cantilevers he will save six ounces or so in weight. Although these brakes are cheaper than their bolt-on counterparts, the cost of brazing on the bosses has to be taken into account.

Hub brakes can be useful at the rear of touring tandems, and these might be fitted with friction damped levers so that they can be set for a long mountain descent, and used in conjunction with rim brakes. Tricycle riders also have a problem and a hub brake at the front, two at the rear, or Higgins' solution of some years ago, which comprised a differential and a transmission hub brake, might help. But these are specialist problems and for the solo rider hub and coaster brakes can be ignored.

Careful fitting of the brakes will be rewarded by smoother braking, by the levers springing back smartly and by a reduction in cable wear. Most brakes will accommodate the different stirrup depths of frames, but C.L.B. make a side-pull for juvenile bicycles, and some Italian frames,

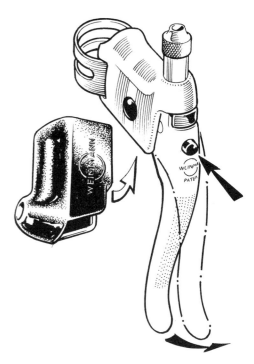

Weinmann brake lever with its rubber hood. It incorporates a quick-release button.

These Mafac Guidonnet levers are well suited to the Randonneur bars, and make riding with a cape easier.

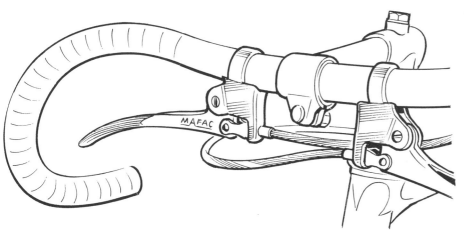

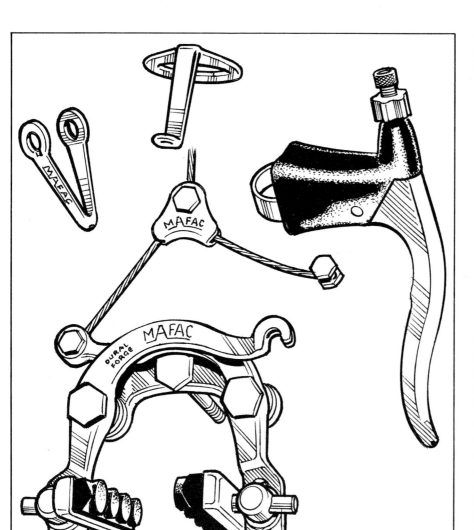

these cables are tinned to prevent fraying, and if after fitting they are much too long, the neatest solution is to tin an inch or so below the clamp, and cut off the surplus. Positioning levers is to some extent a matter of personal choice: they should be high enough to provide a comfortable rest for the hands when riding on the tops of the bars, but not so high that they are difficult to reach when one is down on the hooks. At its best, the modern bicycle is a fine example of applied ergonomics, but get the bits and pieces a little out of place, and it can become a nightmare.

Maintaining the efficiency of brakes entails first checking the tightness of attachment bolts and cable clamps. Cables should be greased where they enter holes and checked for fraying at the same time. A drop of oil on pivot points and a light smear of oil on steel parts like quick release levers (to guard against rust) should complete the preventative maintenance. The brake blocks will not last for ever for if they did the rubber would become too hard (which reminds me of the past again!). When the knobs or slots have nearly worn flat they must be changed, and the new ones done up tightly once their correct position has been found. If you use mudguards but decide to take them off, replace those brake nuts immediately before you forget.

which are shallower than most, may need measuring before the brakes are bought. When bolting on mechanisms, make sure that the closed ends of the brake shoes face forward. If they do not, braking forces will shoot the blocks out of their seatings. When side-pull types have been centred so that the block-to-rim distance is equal, and the levers are pulled and released, one block might still touch the rim. The cure lies in slackening off the attachment bolt, resetting the brake so that the rubbing block has more clearance than its mate, and re-tightening the nut. Apply the brake, and with luck it will go back to a central position. One or two trial goes may be necessary before success is achieved. A brake which rubs slightly is not to be tolerated. Clearance between rim and block should be about ¼in. Make sure that the mounting bolts are tight. The

front one is particularly important for if the nut fell off, braking action would pull out the brake with nasty consequences.

Cables can be completely enclosed, and therefore protected from moisture as they run back to the rear brake, and held on by clips, or run through bosses brazed to the frame. The latter system looks neater, and who wants clips scraping the paint off a frame? But they do need more attention. Where wires pass through the bosses, grease must be applied and before feeding wires or cables through any holes either in cable shrouds or bosses, a little attention with a small round file to remove any rough spots is worthwhile. These are the places where cables can start to fray. If cables are greased before feeding them through shrouds, this will make for smoother operation and cut down the risk of corrosion. The ends of

Saddles

If you use your bicycle to ride around the neighbourhood then this chapter might not concern you too much, but if, as I hope, it will be ridden farther afield, the subject of saddles should be taken seriously. There is a wide range of shapes to choose from, in both leather and plastic. With the latter you even get a choice of colour. Unless a rider is a rather strange shape, he would do well to follow the choice of men who ride long distances. The dedicated tourist usually ends up with almost the same equipment as the road racing riders, who just cannot afford to be uncomfortable.

What, then, is the choice? On one side there are superbly crafted leather saddles which after some riding will become supple, and of course will not retain moisture on their surface. There are cheaper leather saddles which might appear to be bargains, but if the tops are not good enough to hold their shape, and if the frames are not as robust as they might be, they are best left alone. The best leather saddles are more expensive than the highest quality plastic types. If you choose the former, and at a later date decide to sell the bicycle, it is more than likely that you will not part with the saddle.

That hardly sounds like a recommendation for plastic saddles, but the better ones, like the Milremo Super de Luxe are in fact covered with foam and leather. Track and short distance riders would certainly be at home with these saddles, which are lighter than their leather counterparts. A Unica plastic saddle will weigh about 12oz whereas the Ideale leather type weighs $17\frac{1}{2}$oz, and the Brooks Professional, which does not use an alloy frame,

weighs 25oz. A bicycle that is going to be used for local trips, and perhaps be left out in the rain, is certainly in need of this type of equipment, but not one of the kind with fancy tops. The better plastic saddles have gained wide acceptance in recent years. It is said that by not being porous they cannot harbour germs, and certainly they ought to hold their shape. My preference for leather is really based on the fact that my saddles have been so good that I have never had the desire to change them.

Leather saddles must be cared for – keeping a good shape is well worth the effort. Never leave it in the rain. There are several plastic covers on the market, but a plas-

Below: The Brooks Professional racing saddle made from high grade butt leather. Bottom: A high grade plastic saddle, the Milremo Super de Luxe has a leather top above the nylon.

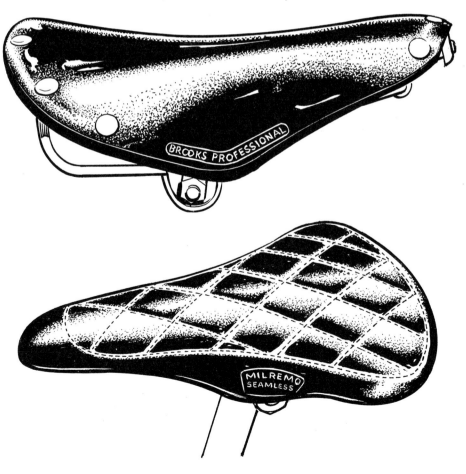

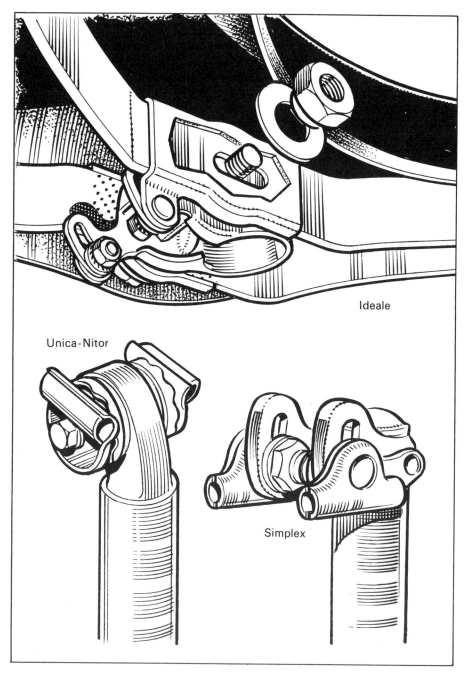

Ideale

Unica-Nitor

Simplex

tic bag and clothes peg will do. When racing on a wet day, a plastic undershield will keep splashes from the back wheel at bay. Your body will amply cover the top. From time to time a sparing rub of Brooks Proofide on the underside will be all the dressing that is necessary. If a saddle starts to sag, re-tension it without delay by tightening the bolt under its nose. Because of its form of construction the leather saddle has its top riveted to the frame. Take care that these rivets never work loose. The result would be bad for the saddle, and most uncomfortable for you.

Perhaps those sprung affairs which would look more at home on a vintage motor cycle should be mentioned, but only in passing, for there is nothing to recommend them.

Having decided on the type of saddle, it must be attached to the frame in exactly the right position. In the past that was not too easy, because the angular adjustment was limited in settings by serrated washers. Some saddles may still use this method, and one may be lucky in finding the right angle–if not, all is not lost. Get a Campagnolo, Zeus, Simplex or similar adjustable pillar. These have infinitely variable setting facilities.

Three saddle adjusting mechanisms.

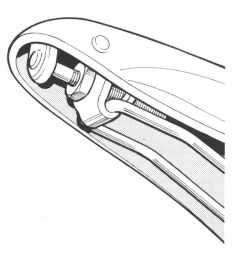

Saddle adjustment is achieved by this nut under its nose.

Pedals

he basic choice here is between ubber and metal. The former ype is convenient if you just ant to hop on the bicycle to ide a couple of blocks. If, however, you would like to ride in the ost efficient manner, then it is ighly desirable, albeit a little nconvenient, that your feet remain in the right place all the ime. So the choice is metal edals, commonly called rat traps, oe clips and straps.

Nevertheless, there is a real lace for rubber pedals. Youngsters learning to ride will need hem. A leg slipping off a rat rap could receive a nasty scratch, nd toe clips are to be avoided ntil real confidence is achieved.

There are three basic types of at trap pedals. The double-sided ype, which when used with clips s really carrying unnecessary

metal, the quill pattern, where the lower side is cut away to increase ground clearance when cornering, and the platform pedal. This last design spreads the load on the feet, and seems to be gaining in popularity. These three designs are all available in steel at the lower end of the price scale from Lyotard, who also make dural quill pedals which will save some 4oz in weight. Campagnolo and Zeus manufacture beautiful models using steel plates, and alloy barrels which are much more expensive. These luxury models I have mentioned incorporate little tongues on the lower edge of their rear plates and these help in flicking the pedals round when putting one's feet in the clips. If you think that is a good idea, but not at the price, then Milremo can provide a plastic version to

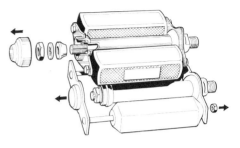

A typical rubber pedal. Underneath an American version, without separate dustcap.

Three representative pedal designs.

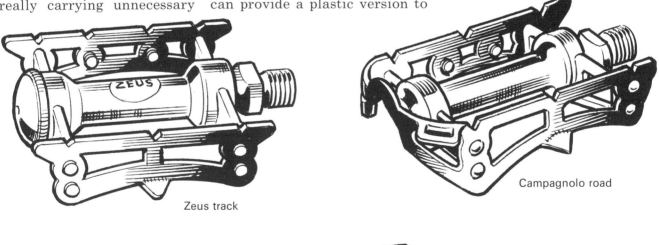

Zeus track

Campagnolo road

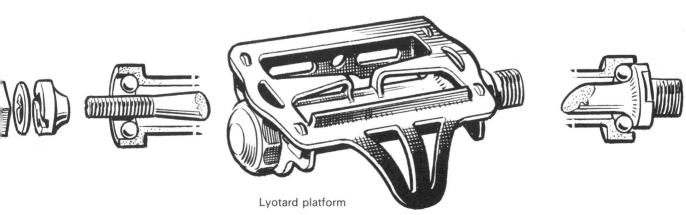

Lyotard platform

fit any pedals, except the platform type which do not need them. If you are careless by nature, it would pay to buy cheaper products and replace them more often, for pedals, being where they are, do come in for knocks.

Several racing pedals are made in slightly narrower designs for track racing. It is important when buying to remember that pedals which are to be used with alloy cranks have a longer thread

riding in winter, those who prefer warm, dry feet, might with advantage fit a pair of Piescho muffs over the clips.

The pleasure of riding can be completely destroyed by badly adjusted pedals, or worse still worn pedals. Adjustment is made at the outer cone bearing, and there should be just a trace of rock when the locking nut is tightened. These bearings need packing with grease to lubricate them and to

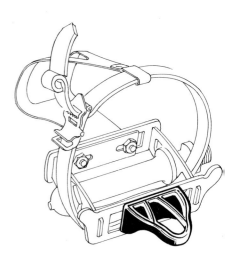

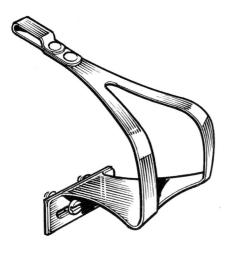

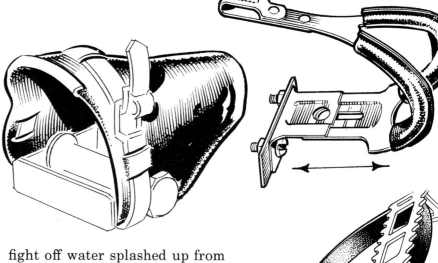

than those designed for steel ones.

Having settled on the pedals, you will need toe clips. These are made in three set lengths, by Christophe, for example. Being manufactured of steel they can stand a lot of abuse. It is possible to buy alloy clips, and adjustable clips, but the fixed steel types take some of the worry out of maintenance. To keep the feet where they should be in these clips, straps are necessary and those with quick-release catches are the only kind to buy. For

fight off water splashed up from the front wheel. When it is necessary to remove a left-hand pedal remember that it has a left-hand thread into the crank. With American rubber pedals it will be necessary to take off the inner plate nuts to get at the bearings; Continental and British designs have removable dust caps to facilitate adjustment. When purchasing new pedals, it is as well to ask if any special tools are needed–Zeus for example make a spanner for dust cap removal without defacement.

Top: This Milremo Rapido pedal tongue helps in flicking the pedal round to the correct angle to slide your foot in.

Centre: Fixed length and adjustable toe clips. The latter is shown with leather pads. The Piescho foot muff helps to keep feet warm and dry in winter.

Above: The tension of this quick-release strap can be released by a flick of the catch.

Handlebars and Stems

Over the years a wide range of handlebar shapes bearing the names of famous riders has been inflicted on the unsuspecting enthusiast; those which survive are closely similar, and with good reason. I remember, for example, trying some bars which sloped rapidly away from the stem, with a very short straight section; when riding with my hands on the tops of the bars, it was not long before my wrists ached. This top position will be used in road is needed in the deeply dropped shapes. For the rest, duralumin is satisfactory. It is light, rigid, and will not rust. The more popular shapes are made in a variety of widths and there is a move towards wider bars which perhaps encourage deeper breathing. It is possible to buy Maes bars in five widths, from $13\frac{3}{4}$in to $16\frac{1}{2}$in, but those riders who feel that this shape is too shallow will easily find suitable alternatives like the Coppi and Anquetil bars.

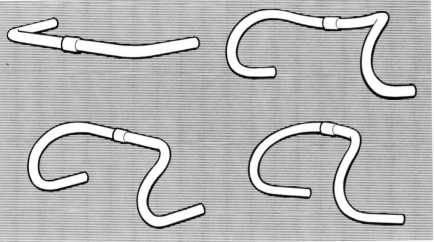

These four handlebars give some idea of the range of shapes. They are Porter, Randonneur, Maes and Pista, for town, touring, road and track respectively.

riding, and tourists will only get down out of the wind when the going is really tough. So for road racing and touring a rather square shape is most likely to be satisfactory. Maes and Franco Belge make typical bars of this type. A bar which has been designed for tourists is the Randonneur, which curves gently upwards from the stem. It is suited to the use of brake levers like the Guidonnet or the Beborex touring model and I am surprised that more tourists do not use them. Track men do not need to consider comfort a great deal, and a little weight can be saved by using a more curved shape.

Steel is the best material for track bars as its greater strength

The ends of handlebars can be lethal in a pile-up, and must be plugged. There are various rubber bungs on the market for this job, and I have hollowed out these on my touring bicycle to take spare dynamo light bulbs. It is a good idea to cover those parts of the bars which your hands will use with one of the special tapes made for the job–I prefer a non-adhesive tape so that there is no risk of stickiness. Some riders who spend long hours in the saddle place rubber pads between the bars and tape to help absorb road shocks.

Handlebar stems are made in both steel and alloy. Some of the latter were too flimsy in the past, so personal prejudice encourages

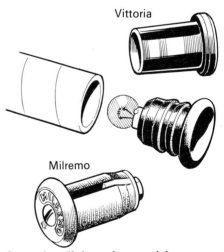

Vittoria

Milremo

Some handlebar plugs, with a handy way of carrying spare bulbs.

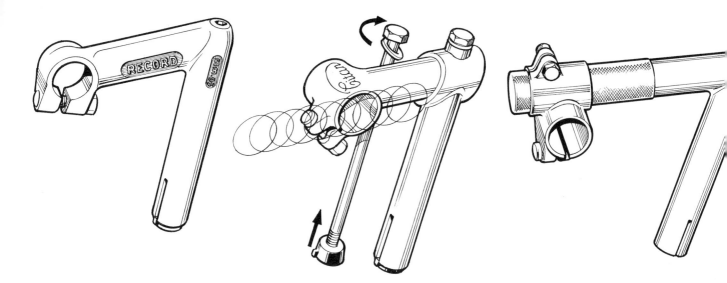

me to use steel ones. The Titan, for example, is made in ten different lengths, which should suit everyone. If a non-ferrous stem is preferred then the choice should lead to equipment like Milremo's dural range, which even in its longest version should be satisfactory. Cyclists who cannot decide on length can obtain adjustable stems, but these should be considered only as a last resort.

The stem is usually held in the fork column by an expander bolt.

Always grease this column before inserting the stem. The other method of attachment employs a head clip, where the column is split instead of the stem. Do not over-tighten the stem—in the event of a crash it is better for the handlebars to twist round than for some part to be strained. Several designs like the Evian Record use a recessed socket head to conceal the expander bolt; this looks neat and is a good safety feature.

Left: An Evian Record alloy stem with recessed pinch bolt screw, and the Titan steel stem, showing the range of sizes. Above: A Cinelli adjustable handlebar stem.

This street in Haarlem, the centre of Holland's flowering bulb industry, would be hopelessly congested if each rider was driving an automobile!

ights

It is certainly desirable that bicycle lighting shows the road ahead, but it is even more important that it gives ample warning of your presence to motorists. As automobile lights become more powerful, the need for larger rear lamps, and better reflectors becomes greater. The choice between battery and dynamo illumination is not straightforward, because both are far from perfect, but can be resolved in most cases by the length of use they are likely to be put to.

Battery lamps stored away in a dry bag are ideal if you are just caught out for a few hours. If, however, spare batteries are needed, the weight is going to be greater than that of a small

dynamo, and one of these should certainly be considered if the bicycle is going to be used often in the dark. Lighting regulations vary from one country to another, but a dual lens lamp by the name of Matex, which straps to the arm, might be all you need to get you home in safety.

If battery lamps are your choice it is as well to pick front and back units which use a common battery size. Because of road vibrations bulbs often shake loose, so keep a check that the rear one is still operating.

As long as you are not riding tubular tyres, there is no reason why a rim dynamo such as the Lucifer should not be satisfactory. The Jos with a duralumin case

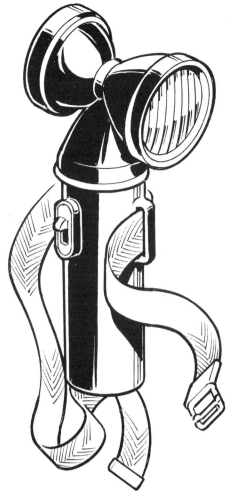

Above: This Matex lamp has two lenses, one of which is red, and can be strapped on the rider's arm.

Below: Front and rear battery lamps.

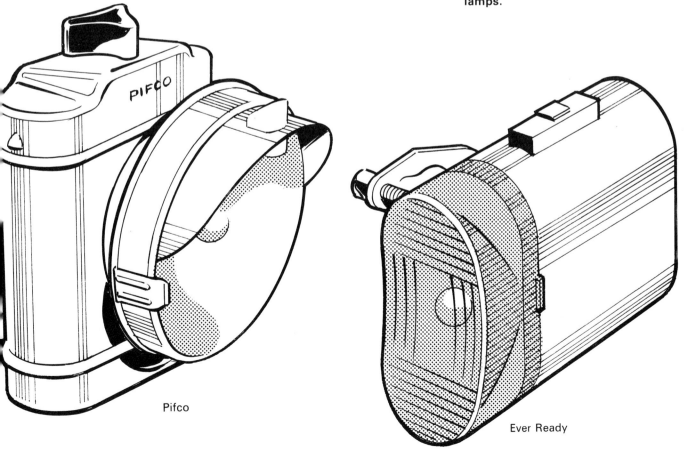

Pifco

Ever Ready

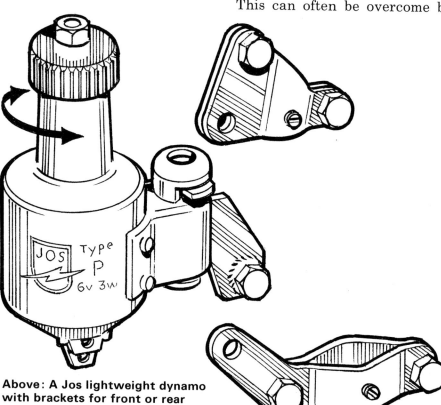

Above: A Jos lightweight dynamo with brackets for front or rear mounting. Its pivot is vertical, and above is shown a typical pulley, useful in wet weather.

Below: Ensure that the dynamo is in line with the centre of the wheel.

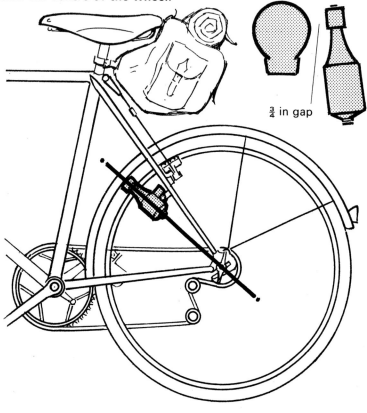

¾ in gap

is very light, and another, the Silma, has separate circuits for each bulb, so there is no risk of the front one blowing if the rear light fails. A disadvantage with some designs lies in their reluctance to rotate happily in the wet. This can often be overcome by slipping a rubber pulley made fo the job over the steel one. second basic type of dynamo i less crude in concept than th rim designs, the Raleigh Dyno hub. This is a generator that ca be fitted either as a front hub, o be incorporated in their wide rati three-speed unit. Of course ther is some drag when it is switche on, but there is no risk of failur to run in rain or snow.

When fitting lamps ensure tha the front unit does point dowr for even bicycle lamps can dazzle The diagram makes it clear hov a dynamo should be set up–it i important that the centre line o the unit is on a radius to the whee centre. Clamps are provided fo attaching the dynamo but strongly advise having a lug brazed on to the frame if it is to be a permanent feature. That wa it cannot slip. On my touring bicycle I have also had small eye brazed on to take the wiring fo both lamps, as this looks mucl neater than clips or bits of tape.

Laws are up-dated from time to time, and thus you could find yourself using out of date equip ment–wherever you are, get ac quainted with the local regula tions. In the U.S.A. bicycles mus have a white lamp in front and red reflector at the back, both o which are visible from 300ft. The reflector must be of an approved type and in addition some states now require reflectors to be fitted to pedals, which should be visible from front and rear at a distance of 200ft. A lamp showing a red light may also be used at the back, and should be visible at 300ft. In Britain the front lamp must be located between 2ft and 3ft 6in high. The rear lamp must be within 20in of the rear of the machine and not less than 1½in diameter. It must be within 1ft 3in and 3ft 6in from the ground, except on small wheel machines like Moultons. Here the mini- mum height is 1ft. A red reflector must also be fitted, but can be combined with the rear lamp. It is permitted to be stationary with- out lights if a dynamo is being used.

Accessories

After spending a substantial sum of money on a lightweight bicycle, the last thing one wants to do is festoon the thing with every goody available. Some of the odds and ends in this chapter will be needed all the time, some of them part of the time, but all of them I hope never. In England most of us are fortunate in not having far to ride to find some sort of a bicycle shop, but for many a mail order specialist may be the best source. Among these are Ron Kitching of Harrogate, Yorkshire–whose catalogue is almost required reading–or in the United States, Cyclo-Pedia, 311 North Mitchell, Cadillac, Michigan 49601, and Wheel Goods Corporation, 2737 Hennepin Avenue, Minneapolis, Minnesota 55408.

INFLATORS are available in a variety of sizes: 18in is the most practical length. The usual way of connecting the pump to a valve is via a flexible connection which should have a deep drilling to clear the valve locking nut on a high pressure unit. Racing men may prefer one of the integral models where the knock-off adapter is built into the pump end. It does save time. Ad Hoc pumps are typical of the metal variety, but if plastic is preferred (and a plastic pump will not dent when used to fight off dogs) Reg make a range in various lengths. If the knock-off device is not fast enough for you, then a compressed nitrogen inflator certainly will be. Milremo make one called Super Corsa, and it will inflate two tyres before it has to be returned for charging. This is most useful to time trialists and massed start men, provided a recharge service is readily available.

MUDGUARDS are unlikely to be seen on a racing bicycle, and where the climate is reliable they can be discarded for much of the year, but riding in normal clothes on wet roads without mudguards is just stupid. Continental designs favour alloy mudguards, and they are strong enough to mount small carriers and lamps. Personally I find them rather noisy as they seem to reflect transmission sounds, and for this reason I prefer celluloid or plastic guards. The front mudguard should have a splash deflector on it to keep your feet dry–attention to details like this make riding in the rain less miserable. The mudguard stays are attached to the fork ends, and there is more vibration here than anywhere else on the frame. If you have trouble with screws coming loose, a tube of the liquid which sets on the thread as they are tightened will solve the problem (this is sold at car and motorcycle accessory shops). If your bicycle has alloy mudguards and you find them noisy, a coating of underseal (from the same source) will 'detune' them.

SADDLEBAGS AND PANNIERS are a necessary evil. After a tour a first ride on an unladen machine is particularly joyful. However, the size of these bags is best kept to a minimum, even if this means touring with bare essentials. For normal day-to-day riding, a small saddlebag is all that is needed–it only has to take a cape, cap, tools, snack, and camera. Some riders prefer a duffle bag, although many hate carrying anything on their backs. However, there is one great advantage to this–if you leave the bicycle for any reason, there is nothing left to steal

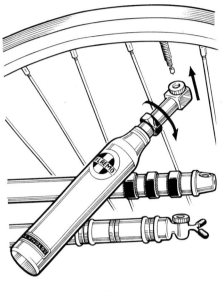

The high speed Milremo Super Corsa nitrogen pump. The Ad Hoc push-on pump also saves time and the Milremo type with horn end rest, even more.

except the machine itself (more of that later). Bellwether make a saddlebag big enough for everyday use, shown alongside a larger European design in the sketch. There are several excellent American bags and panniers available, obviously designed by practical riders.

When it comes to touring and the luggage will not go into one bag, the problem of weight distribution must be solved. My first tour with panniers nearly ended in disaster, because all the weight was at the rear wheel. The trouble did not manifest itself until I was coasting at speed down a long pass; the front wheel started lifting, steering and braking became difficult, and I was lucky to be able to nurse the bicycle away from the rock strewn edges. It was a lesson well learned and I suggest you use a handlebar bag and small panniers rather than the largest panniers available. These handlebar bags, incidentally, are convenient for carrying cameras—it is often possible to stop and take the picture while standing astride the bicycle, when the equipment is stored in front of you. Again, Bellwether make an ideal bag for the job, as is the Gerry bag.

If you are a camper, then the larger panniers will be necessary and Gerry products will come to your aid again. They are available from lightweight camping shops. After a long ride it can be irritating struggling to unhitch bags; TC panniers are quickly detachable, and one half usefully doubles as a rucksack (available from the Touring Cyclist Shop, Box 378, Boulder, Colorado 80302). The Bellwether products are available at dealers or from 1161 Mission Street, San Francisco, California 94103.

Two lightweight Bellwether bags for saddle and handlebar (left), a T.A. handlebar bag, and the large Carradice Camper.

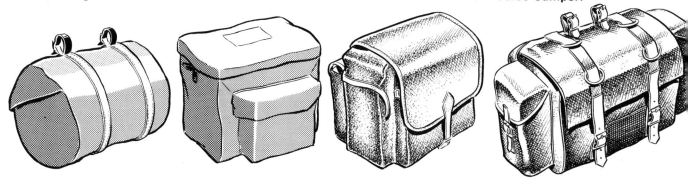

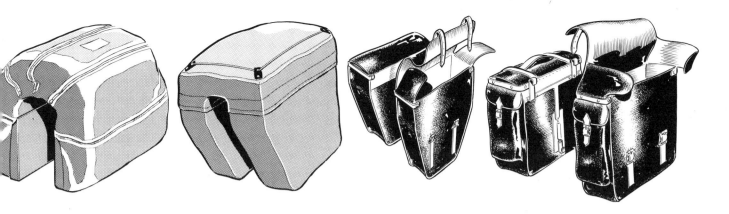

A word of warning to cyclists with big feet: if your bicycle has short chain stays, make certain that large panniers are not going to get in the way of your heels. You will see that the Bellwether bags are angled to follow the line of the seat stays.

Carriers will be needed for panniers and if you have installed the recommended cantilever brakes the front bosses on the fork blades can be utilised for the lower carrier anchorage. Both carriers will probably use the normal brake pivot holes, and the rear one can bolt on to the mudguard eyes. A frame builder can make carriers to fit when he builds a touring bicycle, but there are various proprietary carriers on the market. T.A. supply front carriers which can be used with a bolt-on centre pull brake.

BOTTLES AND CARRIERS are more the province of the massed start rider, but some tourists find them convenient. Two typical carriers are shown and there are many more. A down tube fitting would be useful for a tourist using his handlebars to hang a front bag. During winter riding a hot drink might be wanted and the Reg Thermic plastic bottle is a suitable specialized product (of course it could also be used for

keeping a drink cold in the summer).

TYRE CARRIERS for the racing man help in saving the odd seconds when making a change. The Vittoria unit clamps beneath the saddle, the tubular being held by four rubber strands and a clip. The other carrier shown is a VAR, which is intended to give some protection to both tyre and rider, for it includes a patch of reflective material and is waterproof. These carriers should be used only for the length of the ride, for the delicate construction of good tubulars is not improved by prolonged folding.

FLINT CATCHERS are certainly going to be needed to keep these high grade tubulars in good shape, but they are an advantage whatever tyres are fitted. The idea is that most punctures come after flints have become embedded in the tyre, hammered in by successive revolutions. These devices skim the surface of the tread, and with luck pick off the flints before it is too late. They are attached to the brake attachment bolts on racing bicycles but can easily be fixed on mudguards. If you bolt them at the lowest rear end of the mudguards, dirt collected will not

Left to right: Gerry and Bellwether rear panniers made of lightweight nylon; front and rear panniers made by Holdsworthy.

Following pages: Hugh Porter "Slinging" Klaus Bugdahl in a six-day race. This technique enables a rider to accelerate at a fast rate, when taking over from his partner.

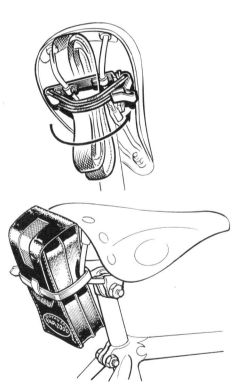

Above: Two carriers for spare tubulars. The Vittoria Fulmine (top), is for racing; the VAR tyre bag does give some protection, and has a reflector sewn on as well.

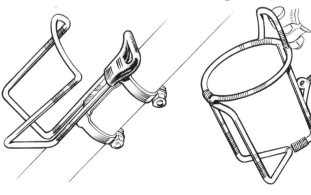

Left: Two typical bottle carriers; one is designed to fit on the down tube, whilst the other is for handlebar mounting.

65

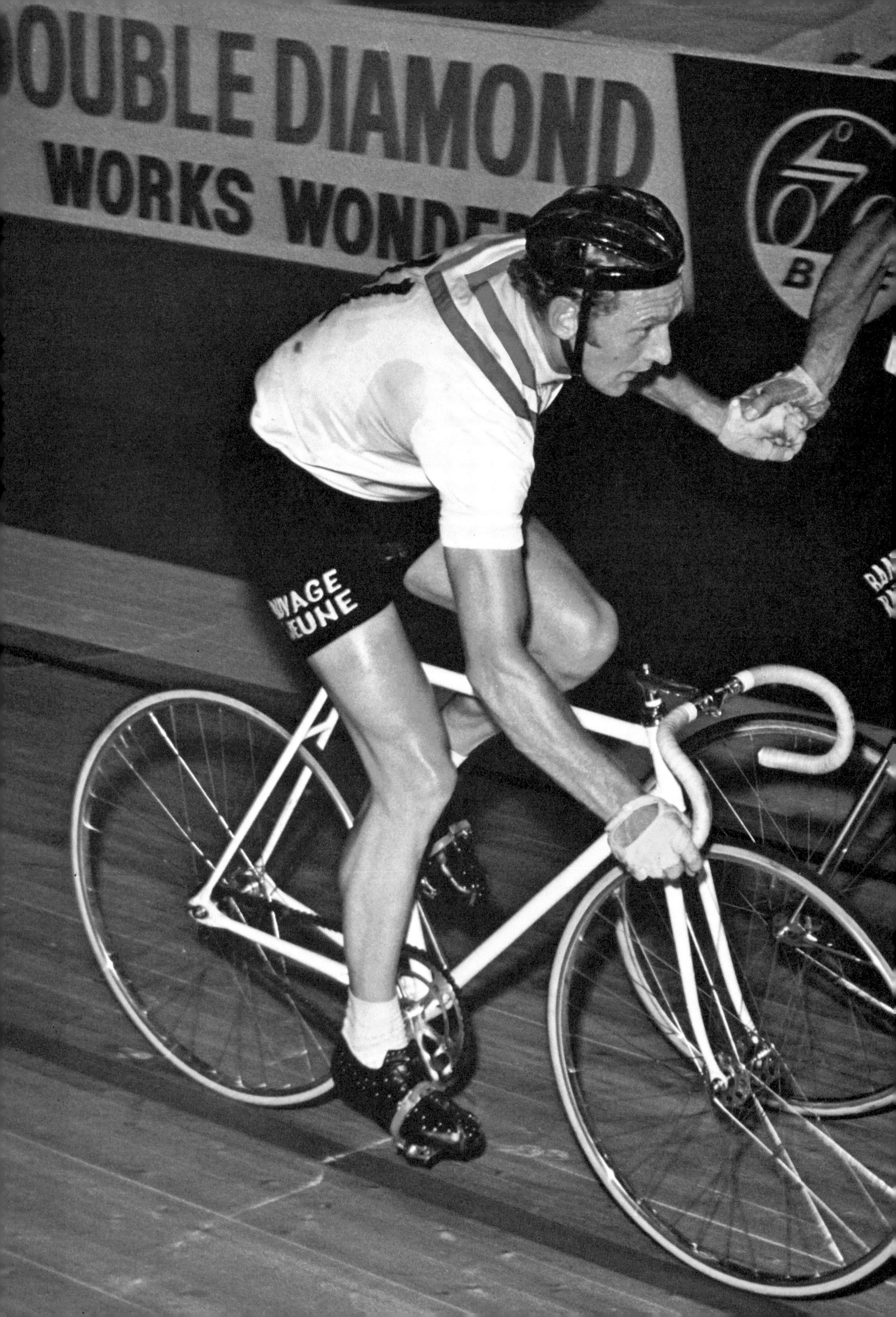

OUBLE DIAMOND
WORKS WONDE

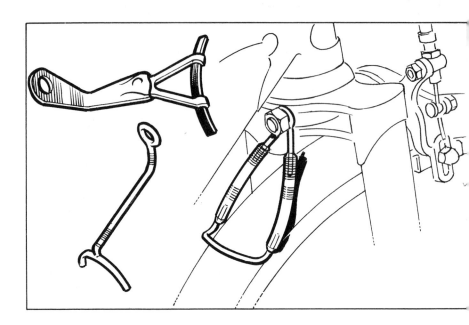

fall on you. The drawing shows
that they are simple devices and
not too difficult to make if proprietary flint catchers cannot be
found.

TOOL KITS need not contain
professional standard spanners,
although these should be used in
a workshop. For occasional ad-
justments which might be necessary there is nothing better than
a Mafac set, but check that your
bicycle does not need any other
sizes for roadside repairs. The
ends of some spanners in the kit
are designed as tyre levers. On
tour I carry a spare rear brake
cable and rear derailleur cable
which of course can be used for
the front units in an emergency.
Being a born pessimist I also carry
a rivet extractor–I have never

needed it but I prefer the weight
to the worry. A derailleur which
is in a very exposed position may
need a special spanner, Campagnolo and Zeus units certainly do,
and it might be as well not to be
caught out.

CABLE SUPPORTS help to make
the bicycle look tidy. The brake
cables need cutting when being
assembled so that the two loops
from the levers reach the same
height. The items illustrated are
useful in keeping them in place.
Something of the sort should not
be beyond your ingenuity to
fabricate if necessary.

CYCLOMETERS are an easier
way of calculating mileage
covered than that of one rider I
know: he counts pedal revo-

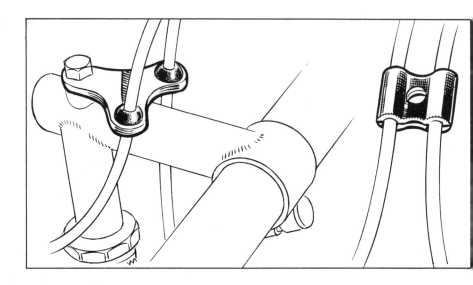

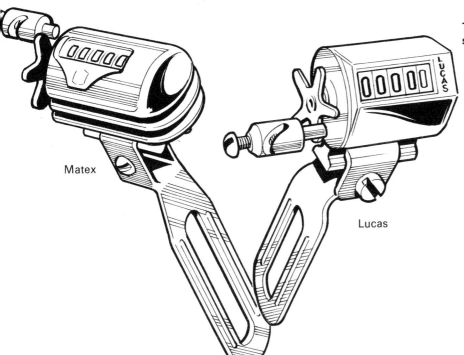

Matex

Lucas

lutions! Those with a statistical approach to the sport will happily put up with the clicking noise as the striker operates (there is one with a wheel made of urethane that is almost silent, the Matex Tour Meter).

HORNS AND BELLS can be a relatively polite way of warning others of your approach, walkers in quiet country lanes for example, who cannot hear a bicycle approaching. A flick of the brake levers or a ping on the bell is all that is necessary, but in other circum-

stances one of the horns illustrated may be preferred. Condor have a range the New York Philharmonic would be proud of.

LOCKS may not prevent a bicycle being stolen but in that unhappy event will enable you to write to your insurance people in all honesty, telling them that you took reasonable precautions. Locks will enable you to chain the frame to a fence so that only the wheels can be removed. A lock will certainly deter the casual thief who perhaps only wants to

get down to the pub before closing time! More you cannot reasonably carry.

BALL RACES to replace worn sets can be a problem for those with little manual dexterity, but others who have perhaps had to rebuild sprocket blocks at the roadside, sticking the balls in place with sun tan lotion, are not easily intimidated. SIM caged races will, however, save one this labour; the ball cages are made of nylon and are available for bottom brackets and steering assemblies.

Some early warning devices. The bell will probably preserve better community relations. Below: A sturdy lock like this will deter the casual thief.

Left: Beryl Burton will be
remembered principally for
fantastic rides against the clock—
her time trial performances are
superior to all but a handful of
men. She is also an outstanding
rider on the track and in road races.

Above: The Tour de France
attracts huge crowds as it passes
through towns—and considerable
advertising revenue from industry.

Roadcraft and Fitness

Most of my riding is in country lanes, and despite the congestion of main routes and towns, these have not changed much in many years. Fortunately most motorists find little joy in map-reading their way along obscure tracks. The sharp contrast between these conditions and the state of affairs in populated areas highlights the need for complete confidence in one's riding ability. To achieve this you must have a bicycle that fits you. The road in front of you speaks a language, and you must understand it. Last but not least, you must be fit enough to enjoy riding. The easiest of these is the first.

The vital dimension when deciding the correct size of frame to use is the inside leg measurement—a rough guide is to subtract 10in from this. My inside leg measures 35in so I need a 25in frame. Because I use a saddlebag for normal riding it is convenient to leave exposed enough seat pin to strap on the bag, but this will be a real problem only for very short riders. Cranks are made in various lengths, the most common being about 6¾in between centres. Shorter riders who pedal lower gears are advised to try 6½in cranks, whilst those pushing bigger gears might need 7in cranks. T.A. cranks are made in nine different lengths which should satisfy everyone, including the short rider for whom the range goes down to 6¼in; Stronglight make their cotterless set in the three normal sizes quoted above; Campagnolo make seven sizes between 6½in and 7³⁄₃₂in.

When deciding how high to fit the saddle, once the frame and cranks are settled, several factors will have to be considered. As well as the height of the saddle, its angle and position in relation to the bracket can be set. As each factor to some extent bears upon the others, a little trial and error will be needed to achieve the correct position. When the foot is at its lowest point the rider's knee should be slightly bent (a little more for a leisurely rider). Some years ago an English university conducted some experiments on the subject and came to the conclusion that the most efficient setting was 109 per cent of the inside leg measurement. My observations show that all my friends have come to this setting by trial and error! If you set the saddle so that this dimension reads from its top to the top of the pedal when this gap is at its greatest you will not be far out. Now the saddle angle normally tilts up a little at the nose, and its front should be 2in–2¼in behind the bottom bracket centre (this can be determined by hanging a weighted string from the saddle). Your weight should be distributed so that the arms

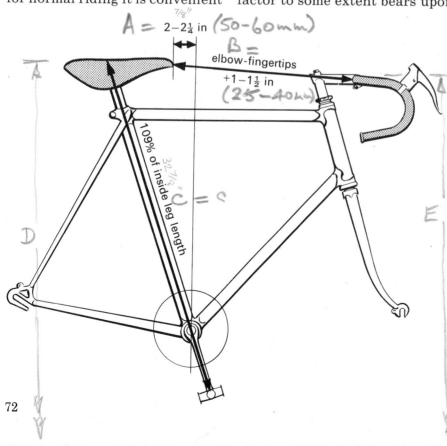

$A = 2-2\frac{1}{4}$ in $(50-60mm)$ 7/8″

$B =$ elbow-fingertips $+1-1\frac{1}{2}$ in $(25-40mm)$

109% of inside leg length 32⅞″ $C = C$

A B C D E

These are the basic settings necessary when fitting your saddle, as angle of tilt is a subtle decision.

INSIDE LEG (IN SOCKS) 790
SHOE SOLE AT BALL OF FOOT 17
807mm
807×1.09=879.63
SAY 880 m.m
DAHON
ATP—11— =880mm
SET BETWEEN 14 & 11

DAHON (M.M.)
A = 62
B = 5
C = 880 – 850
D = 955 – 965
E = 960 (MIN H AVAILA
SEAT TUBE MARK "14"

take a proportion of the load, but not too much. The saddle angle plays a significant part in determining this. The fore and aft setting will vary a little according to the type of riding envisaged. A sprinter will sit more nearly over the bracket than other riders.

Having got the saddle in place, you are in a position to decide on the location of the handlebars. A rough and ready check, handed down by generations of riders, and as yet unapproved by universities, is to place an elbow against the nose of the saddle, and stretch out the arm. Tourists will be happy if their fingertips graze the rear of the bars, while those with athletic ambitions should expect a gap of some 1in–1½in wide.

The bars will also need to be adjusted for height. For touring, the tops of the handlebars will provide a comfortable resting place if at the same level as the saddle top. Racing men will probably need them a little lower, in particular those who indulge in time trials–the need to keep frontal area to an absolute minimum should never be forgotten in this form of racing. But you have not finished with the bars yet. They can be tilted up or down to give a comfortable grip. If the lower grip is horizontal the wrists will not be at a natural angle and aches will result. They should be set initially with the ends sloping down a little towards the rear; they will probably remain that way.

With the handlebars in position you can now decide on the best setting for brake levers. Most of my leisure riding is done with my hands resting gently on the tops of the bars. It is not necessary to grip firmly and pull unless one is cycling up very steep hills, when in any case the levers will probably be held. If they are positioned correctly you will have no difficulty in applying the brakes, whether you are using the top or the lower part of the bars. The bars should not be taped until you have ridden several miles and are satisfied with the settings.

If a frame is fitted with brazed-on gear lever bosses, that settles their position, but if they are to be clipped on there is a temptation to mount them on the top tube. This is not advised. In a normal riding position the hand swings naturally round to grip a down tube mounted lever, and there is also some danger of grazing a knee against a lever on the top tube. If you are not satisfied with either of these positions, there are levers made by Simplex and Campagnolo which fit into the handlebar ends.

To pedal efficiently it is best that feet do not slip about on the pedals. To this end, toe clips and straps are normally used with rat trap pedals. These alone are not enough, however–if feet are simply pushed forward in the clips the toes will become rather uncomfortable. For this reason shoe plates (or cleats) are used. These are rubber or metal in construction, with slots in which the upper rear pedal plate sits. The correct setting will leave a small gap between the front of the shoe and toe clip.

If a bicycle is bought off the peg and it is fitted with toe clips, make sure that these are appropriate to your foot size. The three types, short, medium and long, will cover most cases, but riders with oversize feet might have to fit spacing washers before achieving a comfortable setting. Toe straps will help to keep your feet in position, but should not be done up too tightly. A sprinter or road man about to face a climb will need to have them fitting tightly, but this would be uncomfortable for any length of time. Moreover, when riding through traffic there should be absolutely no delay in getting a foot on the ground, and the time taken to flick the quick-release clips is too great. The technique for removing one's feet, which will soon become second nature, is to lift and pull back.

Having done everything possible to make your bicycle ideal for its task, you must be quite certain that you are also fit for

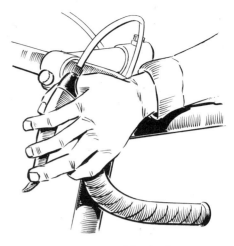

A properly adjusted brake lever can be operated easily from above or below, and provides a good grip when riding out of the saddle.

Following pages: The spectacle of a six-day race–this is an episode in the Skol event in London.

Cyclo-cross spiked shoe plates, and a plastic type which would not be too uncomfortable for the tourist.

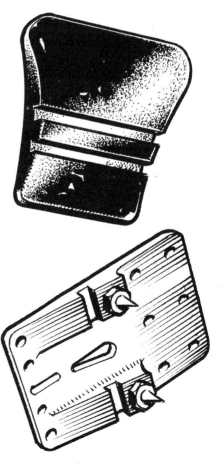

the road. Every state has its own peculiar laws over and above those that apply anywhere, and you must be well versed in them. As you ride along try to think ahead, so that you will be in the right place for any change of direction. It just is not good enough to signal an intention to turn – you must first twist around in the saddle and see if the road is clear, before even changing lanes. This ability to look round is vital, and to do it properly it must be possible to ride with one hand on the top of the bars. Most accidents are caused by road users changing direction. So anticipate a need to turn, see that all is clear behind, give a clear hand signal, and make certain the road ahead is free before turning. In towns with multi-lane highways it is vital to be able to think ahead so as to be in the right lane.

Thinking ahead will also help you to be in the right gear at the right time. For example when approaching an intersection change down while you have a hand free, or when climbing hill change down just before necessary, because the act of switching cogs will slow the bicycle a little and the derailleur system does not work at a standstill (the hub gear has an advantage here). If all your riding is to be in town and gear changing at a standstill appears to be an advantage, then this type of gear might be safer.

Riding after dark can be a problem, for it is quite impossible to match the power of car headlights. Force yourself to look to the side of the road, away from the direct glare. You might try closing the eye nearest to the offending light whilst it is at its brightest. Certainly wearing a cap pulled well down on the car's side helps. It is always important not to ride so close to the edge of the road that you have no room for manoeuvre when the traffic passes close, and at night it is doubly so, because your eyes will take a second or so to recover after being dazzled, and this is quite long enough for you to stray on to the rough.

Having been encouraged to equip your bicycle with really good brakes you should now be encouraged not to use them! Thinking ahead will enable you to coast up to traffic lights or to decelerate to the ideal speed before negotiating a bend, with the barest touch on the brakes. When approaching a corner look at the way the road cambers, for there is usually an ideal line – too tight and you will need to slow sharply, too wide and there will be trouble with reverse camber, and possibly loose gravel. If it is necessary to brake, get it over before turning. It really is bad practice to apply your brakes when travelling in anything but a straight line.

Always use the front brake a little before the rear one. It is very easy to lock the rear wheel, and this is to be avoided at all costs. Obviously you must brake gently in the wet and very gently on ice (remember too that leaves on a wet surface can be almost as bad as ice). At times like this it is important to relax and take it gently and avoid making sharp changes of either speed or direction.

Perhaps the secret of enjoyable riding lies in this ability to relax – having one's body tensed just does not help to get the pedals round. For me, just riding seems to bring about a relaxed state, and worries vanish in the rhythm of pedalling. I think cycling contributes greatly to one's mental health. The more obvious physical side to fitness benefits enormously, but there is a great deal that we can do to help before setting out on the road.

The ambitious racing man will study his diet in great detail and train on at least three days in a week. Even the most leisurely tourist would be well advised to cut down on some of the foods an athlete would do without altogether. The intake of fried foods should be kept to a minimum and so should sugary foods, cakes, pastries and bread. Potatoes, parsnips, haricot beans and peas are of course fattening, and thus do

not help. Grilled beef and poached eggs make a pleasant change but when eating meat cut down on all animal fats. If you enjoy salad and fresh fruit, keeping to a healthy diet should not prove irksome.

If you are going to race, road training should begin at least three months before the first event. Start with fairly short rides of 25–30 miles and always cover the body well with woollen garments. Lightweight windproof clothes are tempting but for training they are not a wise choice because the body cannot breathe adequately in them and become bathed in perspiration. Gradually increase the length of training rides to about 40 miles on three weekdays interspersed with longer trips of 60–70 miles ridden at about 20mph.

Unless you live in a dry climate never ride without mudguards when training. In other respects the bicycle ought to resemble the one you intend to race on. There are plenty of quite cheap tubulars available which are good enough for this purpose. Keep the gears low – do not exceed the middle 70s. After a ride always strip off and shower, or rub down. Once the racing season has arrived weekend training will be unnecessary and weekday riding should take this into account. There is no point arriving at the start tired through excessive training. Steady and well planned training is advised.

One does not expect a touring cyclist to go out training, but I have found that one spin-off from training and racing has been the ability to enjoy the tour without being intimidated by hard conditions. Once you have learned to ride and have achieved a fair state of fitness cycling becomes a wonderfully relaxing sport. Sometimes one cannot ride for a long spell and of course after one of these it would be unwise to go straight out on a long ride. But once acquired, a riding style is not easily lost, and that can be gratifying for it may have taken a long time to develop.

Racing

The first cycle race took place in 1868 at St. Cloud in Paris. It was won by an Englishman, James Moore. The first road race also took place in France, in the following year; this was run between Paris and Rouen and again James Moore was the winner. Soon after this the first cycle tracks were built in Paris and London. Over 100 years have passed, but to most cyclists France is still the home of cycle racing; the sport in France is also a national entertainment and is a vehicle for large-scale advertising. This is not so in Britain where the massed start road race which is so popular on the Continent still attracts fewer competitors than time trials. This is largely because such races were not permitted until comparatively recently, but it is just possible that the idea of a lone ride against the clock, when the best man always wins, appeals to something in the British make-up, as being more of a sporting event.

Because track and road racing are spectacular, and attract the attention of the advertising industry, in Europe they support a healthy band of professionals. This is hardly the case in Britain, while in the United States the sport is largely amateur in status.

Road racing can be divided into two main categories, massed start racing and time trials. The former type of event is usually held on roads and if the race is important these may be closed to other traffic. Some are run on closed circuits, and this form of race is popular in America. Either way all riders start at the same time. In a stage race the riders start together each day of course, their overall times deciding the finishing order. Along the route there are various primes, prizes for the first rider up a mountain or into a certain town for example, and these can help to prevent a race becoming a procession. It is difficult to imagine anything farther removed from a time trial,

This scene from an American road race is reminiscent of the round the houses events popular in France and Belgium.

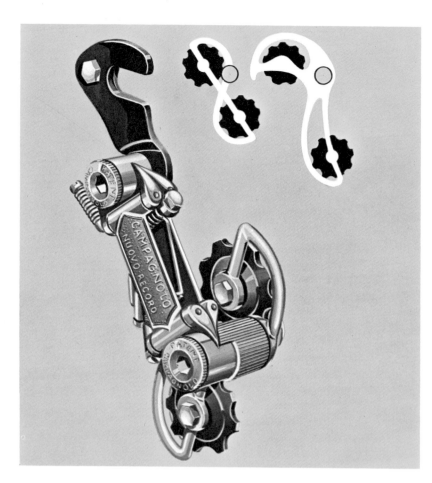

Left: The Campagnolo Nuovo
Record is a fine example of
derailleur design. Inset is a
comparison between the jockey
cage of this gear and the Gran
Tourismo touring derailleur.

Below: These four pneumatic
tyres show the original Dunlop
design, Palmer's cross ply
invention, the Clincher—which was
the first attempt to key the cover
to its rim with air pressure—and
the Fleuss tubeless design.

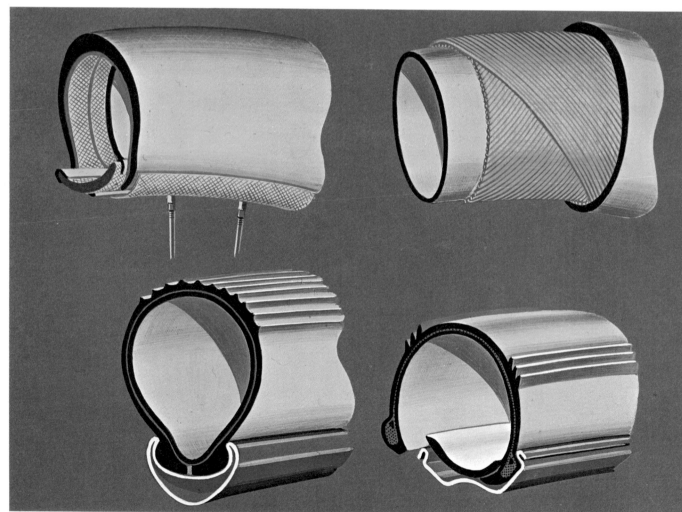

Above: A massed start racing bicycle which would also suit most time trialists.

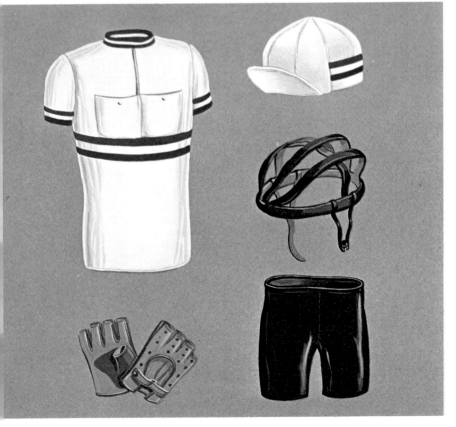

Left: These are some typical racing garments. The jersey would not have pockets when used for track racing. The track mitts are equally practical for the road man, and in races round the houses the crash helmet would be worn by many riders.

Top: Road racing in these conditions calls for great skill in handling when bunched together.

Above: Riders in the Tour de France are followed by mechanics with spare machines, journalists and photographers, and a cavalcade of advertising vehicles.

Right: Sprint racing is the backbone of a track meeting. Dave Rowe in action.

and of the atmosphere which surrounds such a race in Britain.

Whereas road races are not run over specific distances, the British time trial system ensures that out and home courses are measured to the last foot. Races at 25, 50 and 100 miles are held every week throughout the season, all over the country and 12- and 24-hour time trials also play a part

in the programme. Few people in Britain are aware of time trials for most are held early in the morning and are not publicised outside the sport. It is a fine way to compete against fellow cyclists, but is not a branch of the sport calculated to get a cyclist far in international competition. Time trialing is rare in America, where massed start races in fine parks are the most popular form of the sport – they are easier to watch and success could lead logically to international participation.

There are time trial stages in some of the longer European races or 'tours'. Significantly these are rarely won by outsiders. Classic time trials form part of the Continental racing programme, but they are staged between towns, something unheard of in Britain. As well as lone struggles against the clock, 'two-up' and team time trials are held.

Because there can be competition at various levels within one time trial, when riders of different ages and abilities can compete, such events run from time to time are good for the health of a racing club. One can enter with no hope of winning, but with the aim of beating a previous personal best time, settling a personal rivalry or just taking part. There really is not much point in riding round once a massed start field has lapped you. In Britain there is an organisation called the Veteran Time Trials Association, which runs races for riders over 40 years of age–some of its members well past their 70th year still compete regularly.

Cyclo-cross racing also has its origins on the Continent. The sport is held in the winter when

riders are not otherwise engaged and when the terrain is at its most foul. Courses usually consist of short circuits including muddy climbs and descents, rough tracks, a section of good surface and sometimes water to negotiate. This route will be covered several times to make up a distance of up to 15 miles or so, and it is up to the rider to decide whether he is going to ride or run over any particular section. When the sport was in its infancy it tended to be an off-season recreation, but the names appearing in winning lists recently have invariably been those of specialists who reserve their energies for the winter.

Track racing usually takes place on hard surfaced banked circuits which are found in many

European towns (there are seve good examples in the U.S.A.); thi is very much a spectator spor Grass track racing is usuall combined with an athletics mee ing and is not run on a banke track. The track sport falls int two rough divisions, sprintin and pursuit racing. Apart fro the classic two-up sprint match the former activity include three-up and handicap races. Pu suit riders start from diametri ally opposed positions on th track and race over a set distanc in either individual or tea events. Like the road time trialis a pursuit man does not have t develop any sprinting abilitie but must be able to assess h own stamina and spread it with fine degree of judgement over th distance. Madison Square Ga

dens has given its name to a popular form of track racing, for it was here that six-day racing became popular. Such events were originally run on an individual basis with devastating effects on the riders. Two-up six-day races are still common and Madison racing is extremely popular in Europe, where it is known as l'Americaine'. These events are run over various distances and one of the riders in a team must be competing all the time while the other circles the outside edge of the track ready to take over from him.

Tandem racing, various forms of pursuiting and spectacular motor-paced events help to bring variety to track racing, but sadly it has declined in popularity over the years. A small town of some 40,000 inhabitants near my home recently built a superb cycle track and it was not long before the local club had a world class rider among its members. Unfortunately, however, the success of the game is judged by the numbers of spectators it attracts. A larger number of small tracks producing more and better riders might be a more satisfactory state of affairs.

The official governing bodies for bicycle racing in Britain are the Road Time Trials Council, 210 Devonshire Hill Lane, London N17, and the British Cycle Federation, 26 Park Crescent, London W1. The American counterpart is The Amateur Bicycle League of America, 87–96 256th Street, Floral Park, Long Island, New York 11001.

Motor paced racing brings a variety
of different thrills to a track
meeting.

Above: The Holdsworth team in a pursuit race at Herne Hill.

Left: John Atkins, the most outstanding British cyclo-cross rider, traversing one of the unridable sections of a course.

Clothing

Comfort is probably the most important consideration when deciding what garments to wear for a ride. It is quite possible to experience extremes of weather during one outing, and in the course of a long journey of 10–12 hours you may wish that some of the time spent selecting a derailleur had been devoted to choosing more suitable underpants. Whatever you decide to wear, do remember that the position of your body on a bicycle is more demanding than when you are standing in a fitting room.

There are shoes, shorts, various types of trousers and wet weather gear which have been specially designed for cycling, and some useful items can be picked up in climbers' shops. The rest you probably have already.

Perspiration is always a problem, whatever the season. To avoid having a shirt sticking to your back try wearing an open mesh vest, of the kind that is made with large holes. These leave a cushion of air next to the skin, and are comfortable summer and winter. Underpants should be chosen which do not have any thick ridges where they come between you and the saddle. In cold weather, underpants which cover at least part of the upper leg will reduce the risk of chafing.

The most practical form of trouser is the pantaloon. There seems to be little point in spend-

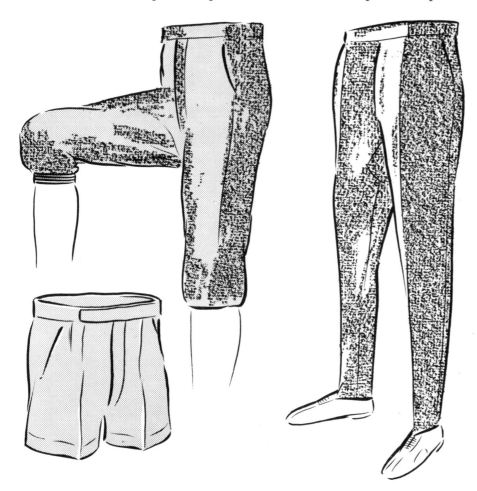

Touring shorts, pantaloons for cold weather, and training trousers.

ing a lot of money on a lightweight chainset and then pumping a mass of hairy tweed up and down. Some riders may prefer the training trousers with narrow zipped legs, which reach down to the shoe. They certainly provide some extra warmth, but at least in damp climates the pantaloon is more practical—when it rains only the stockings will get wet, and if necessary a spare pair of these will not take up much room in the bag. In the past, riders wore plus fours which when wet must have doubled their weight. One or other of the Holdsworthy trousers illustrated is much more sensible. These are made with a reinforced seat and the training trousers are waterproofed. When buying trousers or shorts it pays to make sure that the seams are not bulky.

When it comes to covering the top half of the body, there is often a temptation to wear light clothes under a waterproof anorak in cold conditions. There is much to be said for zip jackets of all kinds, and the climbing fraternity would be lost without windproof outer clothing. However, cyclists should reserve them for the coldest of days, for it is vital that the body is allowed to breathe. It is more practical to vary the number of layers of woollen jerseys according to the conditions and put on or peel off a layer as conditions dictate. When starting out on a frosty morning a sheet of paper under

the top layer, just covering the chest, will keep the wind out, but you will not get that cold clammy feeling that anoraks can induce. Clothing is a personal affair, just as every cyclist's riding pattern may differ, so every rider must experiment for himself. If for example one does stop frequently to nose around during a ride, then a wind proof jacket might be completely satisfactory.

The convenience of man-made fibres is an undoubted blessing and when on tour in the summer, they are useful, particularly when mixed with natural materials. In winter, though, there is no substitute for wool stockings and jerseys. Climbing equipment shops are one of the best sources of all wool stockings and jerseys. Many people can never risk wearing nylon underwear for it can produce a rash on delicate skin. If you do have a sensitive skin, incidentally, a long-sleeved shirt can be invaluable—when the sun beats down all day it is easy to get sore arms.

When selecting shoes remember that they will probably be used for walking around and for that reason the ultra-light racing versions drilled with holes are best avoided. To guard against cold feet in the winter there are fleecy lined bootees—these will at least reduce the discomfort. On a really cold day feet soon warm up if one dismounts and walks along for a few minutes.

Racing men are well catered

Above: This touring tandem has both its rim brakes controlled by one lever. The other operates a hub brake at the rear. The front chain is tensioned by the eccentric front bottom bracket.

Left: Away from main highways, there is still pleasure to be found in bicycle touring.

for, with specialised clothing for every branch of the game. Jerseys for road work are best made of wool of a fine weave, which should not induce too much drag. For long distance racing, pockets are provided for necessities such as food and sun glasses. The rayon and cotton versions, often without pockets, are best reserved for track and short distance road racing.

It is absolutely vital that racing shorts are comfortable. A chamois seat, long legs and a high back should be looked for when buying. The Belgian Alex Sport products are as good as any.

For track racing, a crash helmet is obligatory, and special lightweight road versions are also made. Racing mitts which will greatly reduce the risk of grazed palms in a spill can also be obtained with padding to give some shock protection on long rides.

Most time trialists can remember racing on bitterly cold frosty mornings and a set of woollen arm and leg warmers are to be recommended for these conditions. A training suit which can be quickly removed before the start is ideal for warming up.

Racing shoes must be light and flexible. Made out of supple leather, many now have a steel reinforcing plate in the sole. Some have ventilation holes in both sole and uppers. Cyclo-cross enthusiasts can also use a variation on the winter bootee, which has removable studs incorporated to assist in the 'carrying' sections.

Ankle socks in dazzling white nylon look very smart, but the long-distance rides call for wool, for this helps to cushion the feet, and if you are riding all day every little helps. Feet really are a rider's best friend and should be looked after accordingly; to help toughen mine I wash them in cold water every day of the year.

There is not much that the racing man can do about wet weather. If conditions are really bad at the start, a plastic apron can be worn under a vest – the Belgians use them and they know all about foul weather! There are also plastic racing capes.

The pleasure seeking tourist can afford to take more comprehensive measures; a full cape which covers the handlebars, and everything back to your saddle-bag, is quite efficient if there is no side wind, and if you slow down a little. Long after the rain has stopped feet will still get wet from road spray, and plastic leggings which cover from foot to knee can be worn if this is a worry (personally, I am not too bothered about this problem so long as I keep moving and my body is warm). A cap I find essential, not so much to keep my head dry, but to reduce the volume of water trickling down my neck. Capes can be a problem when a very long handlebar extension is used, and here the tourist who has fitted Guidonnet levers, which clamp transversely across the bars, has an advantage for he does not have to force the cape over the brake levers.

The British style cape, used here with sou'wester and splash guards.

Touring and Camping

The joy of cycling can easily be an end in itself and coupled with a desire to tour the country, it can hardly be improved on. Your hearing, sight and sense of smell are unimpeded. Dull sections can be covered at a fair speed, whilst it is possible to slow down to walking pace without holding up the traffic, if desired. Many riders will want to travel with the minimum of equipment, revelling in long rides through wonderful scenery on lightly laden bicycles but contrarily such tours usually need more organisation than the cycle camper would find necessary. The streak of independence which is strong in most cyclists reaches its peak in campers, but before committing yourself to a heavy financial outlay it is as well to make certain that this really is for you.

Preparation for any kind of tour should start with a close study of maps. The kind given away or sold at negligible cost by fuel companies or national tourist offices will help in deciding which way to point a bicycle, but not much more. In planning a tour, maps which are fully contoured and sufficiently detailed to show tracks are desirable. In Britain, the Ordnance Survey maps to various scales, which are available at many bookshops, can hardly be improved on, while the John Bartholomew 'half-inch' series is also valuable. Bartholomew, 12 Duncan Street, Edinburgh, Scotland and Edward Stanford, 12 Long Acre, London WC2 stock wide ranges of European maps.

In North America the maps produced by the United States Geological Survey are obtainable from the following addresses:

Cycle paths seem to have fallen into disuse in Britain, but are perhaps managed better in America.

Above: A congregation of all ages, astride a variety of bicycles, in one of America's recreational areas.

Top right, right, far right: There is little pleasure in riding through crowded streets, but city dwellers often have access to fine parks where they can cycle free from the noise and fumes of traffic.

East of the Mississippi–US Geological Survey, Washington Distribution Section, 1200 South Eads Street, Arlington, Virginia 22202; West of the Mississippi–US Geological Survey Distribution Section, Federal Center, Denver, Colorado 80225. Canadian maps are obtainable from the Map Distribution Office, Department of Mining and Technical Surveys, 615 Booth Street, Ottawa, Ontario. Rand McNally publish four guides covering Campgrounds, National Parks, Vacations and Mountains and Plains which will help a lot with detail planning.

Keeping weight to a minimum is an art in itself. On one hand there is a slight advantage in taking a nearly empty tube of toothpaste, on the other, photographers have a particular, and real, problem. One of the best cycling photographers I know, who owns a most elaborate collection of equipment, usually restricts himself to one or two lenses, adjusting his brain accordingly. Often his results benefit by this approach.

Apart from basic spares mentioned elsewhere, a first aid outfit should not be forgotten. There are times when hunger strikes at unscheduled intervals, and some chocolate in reserve for these occasions can be reassuring. The need for feeding bottles in races is open to question, but no one is going to be waiting at the road-side for you on tour. I have ridden a 24-hour race without carrying a drink, but I doubt whether I would risk it on holiday.

The question of weight will perhaps influence planning when it comes to deciding stage lengths. In the past I have committed myself to rides which have turned out tougher than some races. Covering 100 miles or so is no great hardship if the route is reasonably flat and not too interesting, but 50–70 miles is usually quite enough if the views are fine, and the churches old.

Weight might even encourage the cycle camper to become more sociable, for much that one person needs will serve just as well for two. There is not much difference in the weight of a tent for one person and a tent for two people, and cooking utensils can be shared–the load carried by each rider thus being reduced by perhaps 6lb.

One of the problems facing the camper is cost versus weight. Fortunately efficiency, which cannot be ignored, acts as a deciding factor. A tent for two persons will weigh about 11lb, less if nylon or terylene is used instead of cotton; Gerry make one with built-in ground and fly sheets which weighs a mere 4lb 8oz but the Alpine Yosemite is more typical at 5lb 14oz. A small stove weighs about 1½lb and there is much to be said for having two of these. Cooking pans and a col-lapsible water bucket will add another 1lb. Plates, mug, cutlery, and food storage boxes must be added to this.

In some ways the most important camp item is a sleeping bag. The economy of a cheap bag seems particularly stupid in the middle of a cold night. The best form of insulation is down, goose being better than duck. There are plastic foams, like Du Pont's Fibrefill, which are quite satisfactory in summer conditions, but these man-made materials tend to be heavier and more bulky than down. The average rolled size of a sleeping bag will be about 17in × 9in and will weigh about 4lb. There are many good designs like the ones by Alpine and North Face. If economy is necessary the Antarctic range, from New Zealand, and Thomas Black's British designs are probably the answer. Black also makes a tough air bed, and this will add nearly 2lb to the all-up weight. The best sleeping bag will do little to cushion you from the ground, and an air bed is one solution to the problem. Puncturing is a real risk, however, and it could not happen at a worse time. An alternative is in the open cell foam pad, which incidentally should have a waterproof covering.

By this time you may have decided to invest in a trailer! The more hardy types camping in an area where weather is reliable might try a bivouac–it will not

These four tents give some idea of the variety of two-man units available. Black's Itisa is popular in Britain, the others are American, as are the two sleeping bags.

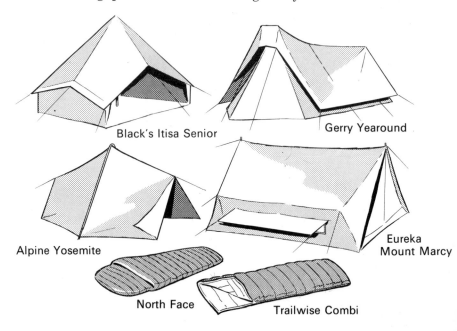

Black's Itisa Senior

Gerry Yearound

Alpine Yosemite

Eureka Mount Marcy

North Face

Trailwise Combi

keep insects out but it is cheap and light. One can easily be made from coated nylon.

A great deal of help can be obtained when organising a tour by becoming a member of one or more of the appropriate organisations. The Cyclists' Touring Club, Cotterell House, 69 Meadrow, Godalming, Surrey, England, organises tours of Britain and Europe: its American counterpart is the League of American Wheelmen Inc, 5118 Foster Avenue, Chicago, Illinois 60630. Membership of the Youth Hostels Association enables tourists to stay cheaply in hostels in many countries. The International Bicycle Touring Society, 846 Prospect Street, La Jolla, California 92037 also organises world tours.

One of the more astonishing feats of the early days of cycling was Thomas Stevens' ride across America in 1884 when he covered 3,700 miles in 103 days on an ordinary. No modern tourist is likely to aim at such an heroic achievement but there is ample satisfaction still to be found in discovering your country on a bicycle. In itself, the joy of bicycling may reveal unsuspected resources of strength and determination.

DAHON 20" WHEELS (19⅛" ROLLING DIAMETER LOADED)

	11	13	15	18	21	24	28	32
53	93.95	79.50	68.90	57.42	49.21	43.06	36.91	32.30
	14.45	10.60	11.48	8.21	6.15	6.15	4.61	

GEAR RATIOS FOR 27in. WHEELS

(ACTUALLY 27¼" ∅ UNLOADED WITH 85 PSI)
(SAY 27" LOADED)

CHAINWHEEL SIZE

SPROCKET SIZE	36	38	40	42	43	44	45	46	47	48	49	50	51	52	53	54
13	74.8	78.9	83.1	87.2	89.3	91.4	93.4	95.5	97.6	99.7	101.8	103.9	105.9	108.0	110.0	112.1
14	69.4	73.3	77.1	81.0	82.9	84.9	86.8	87.7	90.6	92.6	94.5	96.4	98.3	100.3	102.2	104.1
15	64.8	68.4	72.0	75.6	77.4	79.2	81.0	82.8	84.6	86.4	88.2	90.0	91.8	93.6	95.4	97.2
16	60.7	64.1	67.5	70.9	72.5	74.3	75.9	77.6	79.3	81.0	82.7	84.4	86.0	87.8	89.4	91.1
17	57.2	60.3	63.5	66.7	68.3	69.9	71.5	73.1	74.6	76.2	77.8	79.4	81.0	82.6	84.1	85.7
18	54.0	57.0	60.0	63.0	64.5	66.0	67.5	69.0	70.5	72.0	73.5	75.0	76.5	78.0	79.5	81.0
19	51.1	54.0	56.8	59.7	61.0	62.5	64.0	65.4	66.8	68.2	69.6	71.1	72.4	73.9	75.3	76.7
20	48.6	51.3	54.0	56.7	58.1	59.4	60.7	62.1	63.4	64.8	66.2	67.5	68.5	70.2	71.5	72.9
21	46.2	48.9	51.4	54.0	55.2	56.6	57.8	59.1	60.4	61.7	63.0	64.3	65.5	66.9	68.1	69.4
22	44.2	46.6	49.1	51.5	52.7	54.0	55.2	56.5	57.6	58.9	60.1	61.4	62.5	63.8	65.0	66.2
23	42.2	44.6	47.0	49.3	50.4	51.6	52.8	54.0	55.2	56.3	57.5	58.7	59.8	61.0	62.2	63.4
24	40.5	41.8	45.0	47.3	48.3	49.5	50.6	51.8	52.9	54.0	55.1	56.3	57.3	58.5	59.6	60.7
25	38.8	41.0	43.2	45.4	46.4	47.5	48.6	49.7	50.8	51.8	52.9	54.0	55.1	56.2	57.2	58.3
26	37.4	39.5	41.5	43.6	44.6	45.7	46.7	47.8	48.8	49.9	50.9	51.9	53.0	54.0	55.0	56.1
27	36.0	38.0	40.0	42.0	43.0	44.0	45.0	46.0	47.0	48.0	49.0	50.0	51.0	52.0	53.0	54.0
28	34.7	36.6	38.6	40.5	41.4	42.4	43.4	44.4	45.3	46.3	47.2	48.2	49.1	50.1	51.1	52.0
29	33.5	35.4	37.2	39.1	40.0	41.0	41.9	42.8	43.7	44.7	45.6	46.5	47.5	48.4	49.4	50.3
30	32.4	34.2	36.0	37.8	38.7	39.6	40.5	41.4	42.3	43.2	44.1	45.0	45.9	46.8	47.7	48.6
36	27.0	28.5	30.0	31.5	32.3	33.0	33.8	34.5	35.3	36.0	36.8	37.5	38.3	39.0	39.8	40.5
32	30.4	32.1	33.8	35.4	36.3	37.1	38.0	38.8	39.7	40.5	41.3	42.2	43.0	43.9	44.7	45.6

Index

Wheels   F 32 spokes   R 40 spokes.
Chainwheel   50 & 46
Sprockets   22, 20, 18, 16, 14
Crank   6 9/16"
Frame   23"
Leg (inside) 28¼" × 1.09 = 30.8
    ankle
    (. to floor) 31" × 1.09 = 33.8

Raleigh Clubman.
Chain wheels 48, 51
Sprockets   14, 16, 18, 20, 22,
54, 57, 59, 63, 65, 69, 72, 77, 81
                            86, 93, 9

FEB 1998.

Chain wheels   51, 46

Sprockets   14, 17, 21, 24, 28
           5   8   7   7   8 7
39, 43, 44, 49 52, 57, 59, 66, 73, 81, 8
              6   8   5   9

GOOD LOW   EVEN SPREA
COGS WITH   AND EASY
EITHER   CHANGES IN
CHAIN WHEEL   TOURING RA